D1531345

First published in 2000 (as *Classic Gin*)

Second, revised edition published in 2015
(as *Gin: A Toast to the Most Aromatic of Spirits*)

This edition first published in 2018

Copyright © Carlton Books Limited 2000, 2015, 2018

Carlton Books Limited
20 Mortimer Street
London W1T 3JW

A CIP catalogue record for this book is available from the British Library

ISBN: 978-1-78739-118-5

Editor: Martin Corteel
Designer: Luke Griffin
Picture research: Paul Langan
Production: Lisa Cook

Printed in China

MEASUREMENT CONVERSIONS

(Millilitres to Fluid ounces [UK])	
	60 ml = 2 fl oz
	75 ml = 2⅔ fl oz
	80 ml = 2¾ fl oz
10 ml = ⅓ fl oz	90 ml = 3¼ fl oz
20 ml = ⅔ fl oz	100 ml = 3½ fl oz
30 ml = 1 fl oz	125 ml = 4⅓ fl oz
40 ml = 1⅓ fl oz	150 ml = 5¼ fl oz
50 ml = 1¾ fl oz	200 ml = 7 fl oz

GIN

THE ESSENTIAL GUIDE FOR GIN AFICIONADOS

GERALDINE COATES

CARLTON
BOOKS

CONTENTS

RIGHT: *Manufactured in Germany and named after the Siren of the Rhine, the Lorelei Still of Cotswolds Distillery in Shipston-on-Stour, Warwickshire.*

INTRODUCTION

Only if you happened to have been a castaway on a remote island would you not have noticed what's been happening to gin over the last few years. The image of gin has changed or, should we say, changed again.

Descended from the alchemist's laboratory, gin first made its presence felt at the dawn of European commercial distilling when the marriage of grain spirit and juniper was celebrated in the Low Countries. It saw battle as the "Dutch Courage" given to steady nerves in battle and it accompanied William of Orange to the British throne in the Glorious Revolution. Gin has had its ups and downs and the infamous 18th century Gin Craze was undoubtedly a low point. But gin escaped the slums of London and, in the 19th century, was transformed by London's gentlemen distillers into London Dry. Thus began its meteoric rise to become the epitome of sophistication during its glory days of cocktails, jazz and Bright Young Things not to mention the three-martini lunch of Mad Men. However, in the latter part of the 20th century gin slowly fell out of favour.

It's back now. Currently there is another Gin Craze quite different from the first: driven by creativity, new brands emerge it seems almost weekly, new flavours are experimented with and gin has regained its rightful place as the star of a new golden age of cocktails.

Everyone has his or her own story about gin. Mine started early as almost every sip of liquid I had as a child was from a Gordon's Gin bottle. This was not because my parents were irresponsible drunks but because, in Sri Lanka where I grew up, our water was filtered then stored in Gordon's bottles in the fridge.

was psychologically programmed to be a gin lover and this book is for my fellow gin lovers. It's designed to help you find out more about gin: its fascinating history, how it's made, the best gin brands old and new and new ways of drinking our favourite spirit.

EARLY HISTORY

❦

Distilling to make alcohol goes back to the dawn of time but sadly we have very few names and almost no pack-drill. The earliest recorded distillers were probably the Babylonians who, in the second millennium BC, used clay pots to extract small amounts of distilled alcohol through natural cooling for perfumes.

THE FIRST DISTILLERS

Eight centuries before Christ, the Chinese were making *sautchoo* from fermented rice alcohol, the Tatars were producing *arika* from fermented mare's milk and the Singhalese were distilling *arrack* from coconut toddy.

In around 300 AD there began to be written records of distillation – notably those of Zosimos of Panopolis who described the techniques of the fabled alchemist Maria the Jewess, believed to have invented distillation. For centuries alchemy and distillation were inextricably linked in the quest to find the "philosopher's stone", a legendary substance believed to be capable of turning base metals into gold and an elixir of life to achieve immortality.

The European tradition of distilling in an alembic still to make potable spirit almost certainly descended from the writings of Arab alchemists who had translated the earliest Greek and Roman texts. Jabir Ibn Hayyan (721–815 AD), aka Geber, in particular is credited with perfecting the alembic still, which was a crucial tool in his constant scientific experimentation. (The words al-embic and al-kohol are Arabic.)

In the ninth century we find Rhazes, an Arab physician, detailing the use of distilled alcohol as a medium for medicinal herbs and berries. During the Moorish occupation of Spain, Arabic scientific and medical knowledge spread throughout southern Europe via the great monastic houses, then the only centres of learning and knowledge.

In the 11th century, the Benedictine monks at the famous medical school of Salerno in Italy drew on the records of Greek and Arab scholars to create medicines based on combining spirit with various herbs, spices, berries and roots. The Salerno monks specified the uses of these natural remedies and described them as being made with *aqua ardens* (burning water, ie spirit) in the *Compendium Salerni*, one of the first medical reference books. Sadly, they wrote their production methods in code, so there are no surviving recipes. But it is almost certain that, because juniper grows so rampantly all over Italy, they would have developed a juniper remedy, particularly as juniper was used widely in the treatment of kidney and bladder diseases. So the most likely candidate as the first producer of a proto-gin appears to be an anonymous monk in the kitchens of a Benedictine monastery in about 1050.

Arnold de Villa Nova, a 13th-century alchemist, is credited as the Father of Distilling and wrote in his *Boke of Wine* of the distillation of wine into *aqua vitae*. His description, the water of life, now is in every European language: *eau de vie* in French, *agua ardente* in Italian, *usquebaugh* in Gaelic (from whence comes "whisky").

The rebirth of European distilling took place in the kitchens of mediaeval monasteries and great noble houses and it was almost exclusively concentrated on the manufacture of medicinal cordials and liqueurs. A stillatory (a small still) was a standard piece of kitchen equipment and domestic duties included the production of cordials and liqueurs to be drunk as tonics. The therapeutic vlaue of juniper was now wideley recognized and indeed recipes for juniper cordials survive.

Evidence that knowledge of juniper-based medicines had reached the Low Countries comes in 1269, when Flemish poet Jacob van Maerlant te Damme wrote about them in *Der Naturen Bloeme*, a natural history encyclopaedia. Later, Antoine de Bourbon, a French aristocrat, invented another proto-gin. Made from a distilled spirit of wine mixed with juniper berries, it became known as "the wine of the poor". Tantalizing though these glimpses into gin's origins are, we are still far removed from a true gin – that is, a grain spirit flavoured with juniper. These juniper-flavoured drinks were based on a distillation of wine. But in the cold, dank, vineless climates of northern Europe, it was a different story.

LEFT: *The rebirth of European distilling took place in the kitchens of mediaeval monasteries.*

DISTILLING WITH GRAIN

By the 14th century it was generally realized that potable spirits could be made from local crops such as potatoes, rye or barley. At the same time, ordinary people discovered spirits, firstly as a way to make use of an abundant harvest in times of plenty and secondly as a foolproof method of mitigating the harshness of lives that were all too often nasty, brutish and short. From now on, it becomes possible to chronicle the evolution of European spirits from cottage industries to proud national symbols – vodka in Russia and Poland, whisky in Scotland and Ireland, brandy in France and, importantly for this story, genever in the Low Countries.

BELOW: *Amsterdam was the major port through which sugar and spices entered northern Europe from the East and West Indies. It soon became a centre for distilling, chiefly liqueurs, and in a smaller way, genever.*

In the Low Countries, an area that encompassed modern-day Holland, Belgium and parts of northern France, *brandewijn*, meaning "burnt wine", became the catch-all term for all kinds of spirit. Excise records from 1492 indicate that substantial quantities of grain spirit made from local rye were already being produced.

GRAIN MEETS JUNIPER

From the early 1500s, numerous records exist of the regulations and taxes imposed on distilleries that were making this grain

De Harinck-packers Tooren.

spirit. Constant experimentation was carried out to find a way of masking the fusel oil flavours of *brandewijn* to make it more palatable. Juniper combined well with it, particularly when sweetened with sugar, grew everywhere and was considered to be restorative and life-giving. And so genever, from the Dutch word for juniper, came into being. It was a marriage of the tradition of making alcohol from crops in the field to drink for pleasure and the monastic tradition of experimenting with different ingredients to create medicines.

The first written record of genever as a distilled beverage flavoured with juniper was in 1552, in a book called *Een Constelijck Distileerboec* by Antwerp-based Philippus Hermanni. That's not to say there are no other references yet to be found and no doubt diligent historians will keep looking.

One reason why genever was soon established as the national drink of the Low Countries was that a national distilling industry and a huge export trade rapidly developed. Between 1500 and 1700, distilleries were established in every town and distilling became as distinctively Dutch as cheese-making.

Foreigners claimed that it was the foul climate of the Low Countries that made drinking so much a part of life but there were other reasons. The innate Dutch inventiveness and love of experimentation meant that there was virtually no ingredient that they would not distil into strong drink. Crucially, there was a surplus of the ingredients distillers needed. The Dutch had a vast maritime empire based on trade and, every hour of every day, the ships of the East India Company (the famous VOC) unloaded precious cargoes of goods and foodstuffs from all over the world at the ports of the Low Countries.

In return the Dutch carried spirits, cognac, which they had virtually invented, as a way to transport wine in spirit form on long sea voyages, and genever, their home-grown spirit, everywhere.

In the 16th century Amsterdam became the pre-eminent port for sugar and spices and a centre for liqueur-making. Rotterdam was the grain port and Schiedam, its satellite town, became the hub of genever production. Genever is proportionately still the most-exported spirit in commercial history. By 1792, the Dutch were selling 4.2 million gallons of genever abroad annually.

THE ENGLISH ENCOUNTER GENEVER

The English were introduced to genever during the 80 Years War (1568–1648) when the armies of France, England and Spain fought over religion, politics and territory in the Low Countries. Here, English mercenaries were introduced to the local grog, given to steady their nerves before battle. They christened it "Dutch Courage". Later even the great Duke of Marlborough recommended its use "when they were going any time to engage the enemy", and great victories like Blenheim in 1704 and Ramillies in 1706 were credited to its powerful effects. When English soldiers and sailors returned to "Blighty" they usually brought their genever habit with them.

In 1570, London had become home to 6,000 Flemish Protestant refugees so already genever was not unknown in England. Indeed, thousands of gallons of Dutch genever were imported to England in the 17th century – legally and illegally – but it was not until the end of the century that the English officially became a nation of spirits drinkers.

In England spirits had been distilled in a small way since Tudor times. Whisky production was confined to Scotland and Ireland but, because the English had always relied on cheap imports of French brandy, large-scale domestic distilling concerns had never developed at this time.

However a petition to Parliament in 1621 gives us an idea of the purpose of the English distilling industry in that it supplied

RIGHT: *The River Thames around London Bridge was always busy as genever importers sailed into London and delivered their goods at dozens of the city's riverside docks.*

"those that be aged and weak in time of sudden qualms and pangs" and the "King's ships and merchant ships for use shipboard and for the sale to foreign nations". There were almost 200 small businesses in London and Westminster making *aqua vitae* and "other strong and hott waters" for medicinal purposes. Distilling became regulated when, in 1638, Sir Theodore De Mayerne, a physician and alchemist, founded the Company of Distillers. It received a Royal Charter that gave a monopoly to members of the Company to distil spirits and vinegar in London and within a radius of 21 miles. The Company codified the required methods of distillation and the rules governing its practice. This monopoly and the quality standards that accompanied it were swept away in the Distilling Act of 1690 but returned later. Today the Worshipful Company of Distillers is still one of the City of London's most important institutions, engaged in protecting distillers' interests and in many trade and charitable activities.

ABOVE: *Samuel Pepys (1633–1703) was an English naval administrator and MP who is now most famous for the diary he kept in which he chronicled the great events of his time such as the Great Fire of London in 1666.*

Although there were sporadic outbursts of alarm at spirit-drinking amongst young men about town, strong water was still mostly medicinal – indeed, it was common practice to carry a supply of spirit in small flasks for use as a restorative. Samuel Pepys, a renowned social commentator, noted in his diary entry of 10 October 1663 that "Sir W. Batten did advise me to take some juniper water ... strong water made of juniper" as a cure for the indigestion that was plaguing him. The fact that Pepys, well-known man of fashion and *bon viveur*, considered these "hot waters" as purely therapeutic is a reliable sign that they had not yet evolved into social drinks. As the century wore on, we see spirits and what were known as distilled cordial waters, the forerunners of liqueurs, begin to be transformed from medicine into drinks that were drunk for pleasure. After all, what worked as a cure for indigestion could then easily be offered as a *digestif* after a large meal.

GIN'S GLORIOUS REVOLUTION

What changed things was the arrival of a Dutchman on the English throne. In 1688, the year of the Glorious Revolution, the unpopular Stuart king, James II was replaced by the Protestant William of Orange who was married to Mary, James's daughter. The most immediate result was that everything Catholic and French was out, all things Protestant and Dutch were in.

A powerful cabal of landowners, many of whom had helped William to the throne, pushed the 1690 Distilling Act through Parliament. It was to have an enormous impact on the drinking habits of centuries by introducing legislation to ban French imports of wine and brandy and encouraging the distillation of "good and wholesome brandies, *aqua vitae* and spirits, drawn and made from malted corn".

The Act created the economic conditions for an English distilling industry. Farmers and landowners were delighted because it enabled them to sell surplus and substandard crops at a profit. It also negated the monopoly of the Worshipful Company of Distillers. From now on distilling was open to all, once a public notice of the intention to distil had been posted for at least 10 days.

Other strategic pieces of legislation gave a further boost to the development of the distilling industry. The raising of taxes on beer in 1694 made spirits cheaper than beer for the first time, whilst the 1720 Mutiny Act excused tradesmen who were distillers from having soldiers billeted on them – even more of an encouragement.

There was clearly now every reason for distilling in early-18th-century England to flourish, but why that new industry should have flung itself so wholeheartedly into the production of gin, or Geneva as it was then called, is not so obvious. At its most simple England's headlong rush into the years of madness of the Gin Craze was, like many other crazes, fuelled by fashion and greed.

The fashion for drinking Geneva was led by King Billy and his mainly Dutch court. As the poet claimed: "Martial William drank Geneva yet no age could ever boast a braver prince than he …" In the new, more egalitarian, more democratic England that had emerged from the Bloodless

FOLLOWING SPREAD: *One can see how gin came to be called Mother's Ruin in these sarcastic descriptions of drunken "Sweethearts and Wives" by the caricaturist Richard Newton.*

Revolution, drinking this new spirit was a sign of patriotism and Protestantism. It became a symbol of a desire to set aside the old religious and political arguments which had dominated the century, itself now drawing to a close, and to embrace the new wherever it could be found.

Gin's dual nature was manifest from the start. The conditions were already established in which virtually anyone who wished could climb on board the distilling bandwagon and profit from the new fashion for drinking spirits. What could be more of a gift to greedy, unscrupulous distillers than a heavily sweetened drink in which the strong flavour of juniper and other spices could hide a multitude of sins? The stage was set.

BELOW: The succession of a Dutchman, William of Orange, to the English throne secured a place for gin in the national drinking culture.

May we have in our arms what we love
in our hearts... No Tax upon Gin:
Here we go up, up, up... and there we go down, down,
down!

Bless me, is that the Sun or the Mo__
set above there.

I'm a little sickish or so, but no matter...
I've given Sal her gruel: She drinks Gin
with me! Blast me she could as soon swallow
the fat at Landlady!

She's got her quantum, by jingo! She smells as sweet as
daisy! but no matter, I'll get the blunt in the mor__
from her old Goat of a Keeper. For my conscience an__
he will have a precious bed fellow of her to night!

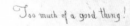
Too much of a good thing!

THE GIN CRAZE

In 1689, English distillers produced around 500,000 gallons of *aqua vitae* mostly for medical use. Less than 50 years after deregulation, London alone produced 20 million gallons of spirits. This figure did not include the vast quantities of illegal spirit: distillers had developed crafty ways to avoid duties by keeping hidden stills and secret tanks.

Honest distillers redistilled this spirit into Dutch-style genever using proper botanicals. But most of it ended up as potent rotgut, often mixed with water and sold in quarter-pints in one of London's many dram-shops for the price of a penny.

This new spirit was called "gin", a word that was originally the upper classes' satirical nickname. Incidentally the first recorded use of the word is found in a political pamphlet published in 1714, entitled, *The Fable of the Bees, or Private Vices, Publick Benefits* by

RIGHT: *Hogarth's* Gin Lane *captures all that was tragic and corrupt in the wake of the unprecedented "Gin Craze".*

Bernard Mandeville, an Anglo Dutch philosopher, appropriately enough. In this satirical study Mandeville writes of "the infamous liquor, the name of which, derived from Juniper berries in Dutch, is now, by frequent use and the Laconick spirit of the Nation shrunk into a Monosyllable, Intoxicating Gin that charms the unactive, the desperate and the crazy of either Sex …".

By the 1720s, the streets of London were awash with cheap, noxious spirit. The slums of St Giles, an urban hell, were gin central as London's poor discovered this new highly addictive drug. This area (behind modern-day Oxford Street where Centre Point now stands) was the setting for William Hogarth's famous engraving *Gin Lane*, a visual parable on the shocking effects of the gin-mania that gripped the city. Here is pictured the slatternly mother, too drunk to notice her child is falling from her arms. Drunkards fight in the street and desperate customers queue at the pawnbrokers in search of money to buy gin. Dangling in the sky is the figure of a bankrupt who has hanged himself. Crowds storm Kilman's, the distillers. Carved above the cellar door below is the famous sign: "Drunk for a penny, dead drunk for tuppence, straw for free."

Hogarth had been inspired to make this powerful piece of propaganda by statistics such as these:

- The death rate in London, in 1723, outstripped the birth rate and remained higher for the next 10 years.
- Between 1730 and 1749, 75% of all the children christened in London were buried before the age of five.
- At one point, there were 7,044 licensed gin retailers in a city of 600,000 people, plus thousands more street vendors peddling the deadly spirit.
- Between the years 1740 and 1742, in London, there were two burials to every baptism.
- The hospices and hospitals in the city were packed with "increasing multitudes of dropsical and consumptive people arising from the effects of spirituous liquors".
- Nine thousand children in London died of alcohol poisoning in 1751.

The whole of London society was scandalized by the story of Judith Dufour, who had taken her two-year-old daughter from the workhouse, strangled her, and sold her clothes to pay for gin. It was extensively reported in the newspapers of the day and contributed to an image of the London poor as a drunken, out-of-control population. Numerous pamphlets and articles denounced gin as the ruin of family life and slowly the demand for reform became unstoppable.

Attempts began to be made to control the gin madness. They were badly thought out – like the one that decreed that only dwelling houses could sell "intoxicating liquors". The Act of 1736 caused the most controversy as it attempted to fix a licence fee of £50 for gin retailers, prohibited the sale of gin in quantities under two gallons and taxed gin at £1 per gallon. The reaction was outrage. This Act inspired poetry and pamphlets and even a long-running theatre show written by Henry Fielding.

On the eve of the Act becoming law there was a night of extreme gin madness. Mock funeral processions took place all over the country, with people carrying effigies of Madam Geneva. In London, taverns painted their punch bowls and signage black and an official funeral for Mother Gin took place in Swallow Street, just off Piccadilly, complete with a horse-drawn funeral carriage and hordes of mourners dressed in black, drinking the last legal gin in copious quantities.

But nothing much changed. In fact, sales of illicit gin – now sardonically called "Parliamentary Brandy" – soared, and in 1742 the Act was repealed.

THE GIN OF THE GIN CRAZE

The only thing that modern gin has in common with the gin of the Gin Craze is the name. Gin had many other nicknames – Madam Geneva, Ladies' Delight, Royal Poverty, My Lady's Eye-water, Kill-Grief, Cock-my-Cap, King Theodore of Corsica and Blue Lightning (because habitual gin-drinkers' faces often turned blue) – to name just a few.

The traditional way of purifying spirit by re-distillation was expensive, time-consuming and required skill, not to mention proper stills and equipment. Setting up a distillery could cost as much as £4,000, a staggering sum in those days. The bootleg-distillers in St Giles and the East End needed much quicker results. So substances like oil of turpentine mimicked the flavour of juniper berries whilst sulphuric acid, rock salt and quick lime were used to purify cheap spirit or "low wine" that had been distilled once or at the most twice. According to the anti-gin crusaders, distillers often threw in rotten fruit, urine and animal bones. Almost certainly they sneaked in hard maltum, a poisonous alkaloid frequently used by nefarious brewers to make beer more inebriating.

AN INDUSTRY IS BORN

In 1743 the government introduced yet another Gin Act. This one achieved a balance between the need to control gin production – urgent now, given that spirit production had reached eight million gallons with only around 40 gallons declared for duty – and pragmatism. Rather than trying to enforce a form of prohibition, Parliament was encouraging the far more realistic goals of control and moderation.

ABOVE: *An inn sign shows the allegorical figure of gin, Madame Geneva, as a burden to the drinking man.*

Spurred on by the success of this Act and a rising anti-gin crusade, Parliament passed a law in 1751, known as the Tippling Act. Only established licensed public houses could now sell gin. If credit was given to customers, sums under £1 were not recoverable in law and those in charge of jails and workhouses were specifically forbidden to retail alcohol.

By further controlling those who could sell gin and by raising excise duties to a level that would discourage the back-street boys, the Tippling Act dragged gin kicking and screaming out of the gutter. Taxes and duties on gin began to produce a valuable source of revenue for the public purse and the excise duty on spirits was raised steadily. Prices rose correspondingly and consumption fell. During the years of bad harvest between 1757 and 1760, all distillation of spirits from grain was prohibited. This had such beneficial effects on public health that there were demands that the prohibition should be permanent. The farmers protested vociferously. A compromise was reached and the duty was raised yet again.

By the closing stages of the 18th century the Gin Craze was virtually over. Ever-increasing excise duties meant gin was no longer cheap. Stricter quality controls led to the proper supervision and management of distilling and drove out the unscrupulous. This encouraged respectable companies to begin to make quality products and it is no coincidence that the rise of the great English distilling houses dates from this time.

London was the centre of the trade and, by 1790, was producing 90% of English gin. As the city with the biggest population, it had never-ending demand but there were many reasons why London was the perfect location for distillers. From its earliest times, the growth and prosperity of London were based on the fact that it had an estuary with a double tide that allowed goods to be brought up the River Thames from the sea into the heart of the city. By the time reputable gin-distilling developed in the late 18th century, London's dockyards had doubled in size and expanded eastwards. Now London was the biggest and busiest port in the world. Tourists came from all over Europe to gaze at the Pool of London and marvel at how it was possible to cross the river by means of the ships moored there. Thanks to the River Thames, the motorway of its time, London's distillers had easy access to the raw ingredients they needed: fruit, spices and herbs brought in by the East India Company; sugar from British colonies in the Caribbean; grain from East Anglia and Kent.

In 1794, there were around 40 distillers, malt distillers and rectifiers, in the cities of London and Westminster, and Southwark, according to one contemporary trade directory. Compare this with 50 years earlier when there were reckoned to be 1,500 in the same area with most owning less than £100-worth of equipment.

Distilling had become big business with a number of London tradespeople dependent on it for their living. A contemporary account describes them as "coopers, backmakers, coppersmiths, wormmakers, smiths, bricklayers, plumbers, all concerned in the coal trade, all employed on the land producing the corn, landlords, those that carry it to the sea or waterside, captains and masters, sailors, bargemen, corn factors, millers and all those involved in bringing in spices, seeds and sugar from abroad". Farmers, too, relied on the distilling trade as it allowed them to sell below-standard grain at a profit. It is estimated that, in the 1820s, around three-quarters of the grain on the London corn market was purchased by distillers.

Because large quantities of clean water are required in the distillation process, many distillers were located in those parts of London that were not only convenient for river transport but also close to sources of pure water. Clerkenwell, the site of an ancient and sacred spring called Clerk's Well, was a distilling hub. It was connected directly to the docks via the River Fleet, then the second-largest river in London.

The introduction of a minimum legal still capacity led to smaller firms, which did not have the resources to invest in production, being swallowed up by larger ones. Gradually the industry became concentrated into fewer hands and, by the 19th century, there were about six large distilling firms and several smaller ones, based in London producing quality products. Of these Booth's and Boord's were the largest producers and Gordon's was already prominent.

Distilling had shaken off its disreputable image. A major sign of social acceptance came when an important distiller, Sir Robert Burnett, was made Sheriff of the City of London in 1794. As the ever-waspish Boswell commented in his *Life of Johnson*, "Foreigners are not a little amazed when they hear of brewers, distillers and men in similar departments of trade held forth as persons of considerable consequence."

LEFT: *Between 1760 and 1815 London's population doubled in size as it became the first "world city".*

OLD TOM GIN

JAMES MELLOR & SON

LIVERPOOL

LONDON DRY GIN

Lord Kinross in his book *The Kindred Spirit* gives a marvellous description of gin as the "ardent spirit which rose from the gutter to become the respectable companion of civilized man". That rise was accomplished through a combination of an evolution in the drink itself together with a broader change in social conditions and attitudes towards drinking. It started in the 19th century.

OLD TOM GIN

At the beginning of the 19th century, the gin sold in barrels to retailers was often accompanied by descriptors such as "Old Tom", "Young Tom", and "Celebrated Cream Gin". What seemed to have happened over time was that, in much the same way as Hoover would later become the common name for any type of vacuum cleaner, Old Tom became the generic name for gin and later evolved into the term distillers used for sweetened gin. In the beginning, however, all gin was sweetened: first, because sugar very effectively masked fusel oil flavours in the base spirit before the invention of the continuous still allowed for a clean neutral spirit to be made; secondly, because popular taste leant towards sweetness. Old Tom was then produced around 25% ABV and was sold in drams in the gin palaces to be drunk neat in shots.

It is believed that Old Tom gin got its name from a certain Captain Dudley Bradstreet, an enterprising bootlegger. When the first spectacularly unsuccessful attempt to control gin sales was made in 1736, he acquired a property on Blue Anchor Lane and invested £13 in gin purchased from Langdale's distillery in Holborn. He set up a painted wooden sign of a cat in the window and broadcast the fact that gin could be purchased "by the cat". Under the cat's paw sign there was a slot and a lead pipe, which was attached to a funnel situated inside the house. Customers placed their money in the slot and duly received their gin. Bradstreet's business prospered until complaints about the "cat-man" became too numerous and competitors emerged. His idea was soon copied all over St Giles where people would stand outside houses, call out "puss" and when the voice within replied "mew", they knew that they could buy bootleg gin inside.

Unlikely as it seems, the story of the bold Captain Bradstreet is probably true. What is certainly true is that by the time branded bottles came in, most brands of Old Tom gin carried an illustration of a black cat.

All the distilling companies produced an Old Tom-style gin until the 1960s when, because of lack of demand, production slowly ceased. Old Tom then became virtually extinct but it's become available again as a number of Old Tom-style gins have launched in response to modern bartenders' desire to create the authentic cocktails of yesteryear. (*See Directory* for details.)

THE CREATION OF LONDON DRY

Throughout the early 19th century, when people drank quality gin, they were usually drinking Old Tom or various types of Geneva or Hollands (all basically copies of Dutch-style genever). By the 1860s, however, heavy, sweet gin began to be displaced by unsweetened, clear gin in what came to be known as the London Dry style. "Dry" because it was unsweetened – "London" because most of the distillers making it were in London.

BELOW: This bottle of Gordon's Special Dry London Gin told the drinker how good it was, being "White for purity" and "free from colouring-matter and all injurious ingredients".

There are several practical reasons why this new style of gin gradually took over. First, of course, was the increasing use of the continuous still that allowed a purer, more consistent spirit to be made. Now the quality of a pure grain spirit could be enhanced with subtle flavours rather than disguised with sugar.

Sugar had arrived in 19th-century London in vast quantities at the West India Dock. Completed in 1802, it was the largest dock complex in the world, the massive £600,000 cost having been paid by the sugar merchants, plantation owners and slave traders who "invested" their profits from the thriving trade in sugar and people.

Secondly, a great disaster overtook London's distillers in the 1870s, when the impact of the dreaded *phylloxera* blight began to be felt. *Phylloxera* was an aphid infestation imported on vine stock shipped from the US to France in 1862, which destroyed most of Europe's vineyards. Consequently, brandy became almost unobtainable.

Distillers at this time made a huge variety of liqueurs using French brandy as well as gin. Cherry brandy, curaçaos, parfait amour, ginger brandy, maraschino, noyeau and others were the big sellers. Suddenly an entire income stream disappeared. Distillers realized that they had to diversify. Whilst some began to bottle Scotch and Irish whiskies as "British liqueurs", others took a long, hard look at gin as demand for it increased among sophisticated drinkers now deprived of brandy. Slowly but surely gin was crawling out of the back streets to become a drink for the affluent middle classes.

DRINKING HABITS IN THE 19TH CENTURY

Gin-drinking did not simply disappear once the Gin Craze ended and the back-street distillers disappeared. The poorest of the poor could no longer afford it but gin still provided solace and comfort to the working poor in large cities like London. Even here gin-drinking was becoming more refined and one of the most popular gin drinks was purl. Originally purl had been ale steeped with herbs such as the tops of wormwood plants and other bitter herbs. By the middle of the 19th century the recipe was to mull ale with gin, sugar and spices such as ginger. It was sold by purl-men from purl-boats on the Thames and in many taverns and alehouses.

However, attitudes towards drink and drinking fundamentally changed during Queen Victoria's long reign. Throughout the previous century one thing those at the top of the social scale and those at the bottom had had in common was a love of excessive drinking. In 1773 the famous Dr Johnson spoke of a time when "all the decent people in Lichfield got drunk every night and were not thought the worse of". By Victoria's time, drunkenness was not socially acceptable amongst the upper classes. Even more importantly, the lower classes were to be actively protected from the evils of drink.

The British Temperance movement started in Preston in Lancashire in 1832 with the signing of the first abstinence pledge. Many thousands signed the pledge at mass rallies and influential people joined the cause. Although the Temperancers never had much political success in Britain, their main achievement was to drive through legislation to control when, how, and by whom alcohol could be sold, much of which was beneficial. Who for example would dispute banning the practice of selling small children "squibs" – child-size portions of gin sold by unscrupulous landlords?

Ironically the failure of the Temperancers to completely ban the sale and consumption of alcohol enshrined the right to drink in British law – encapsulated by the bishop who declared during yet another stormy licensing debate in the House of Lords, "I would rather see England free than England sober." Later, when the Liberal government sought re-election in 1874, it was rejected by voters bitter about Gladstone's capitulations to prohibitionism.

"We have been borne down in a torrent of gin ..." the defeated Gladstone complained.

Spirits were still seen as the problem: drinking beer by comparison was perceived as wholesome and somehow English – at least, until the more hard-line teetotallers entered the fray.

PALACES OF THE PEOPLE

One should never forget that the companion piece to Hogarth's *Gin Lane* was *Beer Street*. In *Beer Street* (reputedly sponsored by a cartel of London brewers) all was quiet, orderly and peaceful. As part of the anti-gin drive, the consumption of beer had been actively encouraged and the number of licensed beer shops proliferated. Many were dirty and ramshackle, so magistrates demanded improvements before granting and renewing licences. Beer-shop owners would often borrow money from the major brewers in order to make the necessary improvements, in return promising to buy supplies exclusively from them. And so began the "tied house" system that was to indirectly have a major effect on gin's rise to respectability.

By 1816 half the victualling houses in London were "tied" and brewers were building even more upmarket premises to draw in the passing trade. Desperate to compete, the seedy gin-shops upped their ante, transforming themselves into oases of glamour, people's palaces where ordinary folk could escape their wretched surroundings. The more sordid and squalid the neighbourhood, the more numerous and luxurious were its gin palaces. There is a contemporary description of one of these by Dickens from *Sketches by Boz* that is so evocative it deserves to be quoted at length:

"You turn the corner. What a change. All is light and brilliancy. The hum of many voices issues from that splendid gin-shop which forms the commencement of the two streets opposite; and the gay building with the fantastically ornamented parapet, the illuminated clock, the plate-glass windows

ABOVE: *William Ewart Gladstone (1809–98) was Prime Minister four times. He blamed the ending of his first term of office on anti-prohibitionists who had opposed his government's attempts to control the sale of alcohol.*

surrounded by stucco rosettes, and its profusion of gas-lights in richly-gilt burners, is perfectly dazzling when contrasted with the dirt and dark we have just left. The interior is even gayer than the exterior. A bar of French-polished mahogany, elegantly-carved, extends the whole width of the place; and there are two side-aisles of great casks, painted green and gold, and bearing such inscriptions as 'Old Tom, 549'; 'Young Tom, 360'; 'Samson, 1421' – the figures agreeing, we presume, with 'gallons', understand. Beyond the bar is a lofty and spacious saloon, full of the same enticing vessels, with a gallery running round it, equally well furnished. On the counter, in addition to the usual spirit apparatus, are two or three little baskets of cakes and biscuits which are carefully secured at the top with wicker-work to prevent their contents being unlawfully extracted."

The success of the gin palaces introduced the idea of drinking as a social activity, not merely a shortcut to oblivion. The first to open in London was probably that of Thompson & Fearon's in Holborn in around 1832. Soon they were a feature of life in industrial cities. (In fact many fine examples remain despite the vandalism of the 1970s – the Barley Mow, the Princess Louise and the Salisbury in London, the Cafe Royal in Edinburgh, the Horseshoe in Glasgow and perhaps one of the most famous bars in the world – the Crown in Belfast, owned by the National Trust which spent over £400,000 to restore it to its original palatial glory.)

Not everyone approved and one only has to look at the drawings of reformed alcoholic George Cruikshank, Dickens's illustrator, for the moralists' point of view.

GIN'S INCREASING RESPECTABILITY

Once the principle of moderate drinking was established in law and the stigma attached to gin-drinking in particular began to disappear, the new essentially middle-class style of gin quickly found middle-class audiences, particularly amongst women. In 1861 off licences to sell alcohol were granted to retailers. By 1872 the Temperance societies were up in arms about "grocers' gin", citing cases like that of the Ipswich shop which sold gallons of gin a week almost exclusively to women. Many of these were genteel Victorian ladies who served gin at tea parties from decanters labelled "Nig", coyly calling it "white wine".

OPPOSITE: *Hogarth's* Beer Street, *where order, quiet and peace preside, is the antithesis of his apocalyptic* Gin Lane.

BEER STREET.

Beer, happy Produce of our Isle
Can sinewy Strength impart,
And wearied with Fatigue and Toil
Can chear each manly Heart.

Labour and Art upheld by Thee
Successfully advance,
We quaff Thy balmy Juice with Glee
And Water leave to France.

Genius of Health, thy grateful Taste
Rivals the Cup of Jove,
And warms each English generous Breast
With Liberty and Love.

GIN AND THE BRITISH EMPIRE

This was also the great age of colonialization when the sun never set on the British Empire. For thousands of expats serving in far-flung outposts, English gin was not just a cure for homesickness, it was a lifesaver – literally. They drank it with another new invention – Indian tonic water – to prevent malaria. When they finally came home they brought the taste for this new, sophisticated drink with them. And, if Rear Vice Admiral (rtd) Jenkins drank gin, it must be all right.

In the 19th century whilst other ranks drank the traditional Navy drink of rum, gin became the drink of officers on British Navy ships. (The same had been true a century earlier on Dutch ships where the officers drank genever, the lower orders rum.) Wherever the Navy went they took gin, sowing the seeds of a huge export trade.

Until the mid-19th century all UK-produced gin was for the domestic market. Heavy excise duties handicapped the export trade until, in 1850, Sir Felix Booth of the Booth distilling family spent a small fortune on pushing a Private Bill through Parliament to remove excise duties on export gin. Orders poured in from every corner of the world, particularly those corners that the British had painted pink. Gordon's, for example, still have a record of a shipment to a group of Australian miners who sent their payment in advance – in gold dust. The reputation of English gin began to travel the world.

The connection between gin and the Navy remains in the "gin pennant", the green and white flag traditionally run up as an invitation to board.

ABOVE: *The British in India were the first to make the connection between gin and tonic water when they livened up their daily anti-malarial with a dash of the London Dry.*

UPWARDLY MOBILE

BELOW: *The publication of Booth's* An Anthology of Cocktails, *in which the cream of society gave their favourite cocktail recipes, firmly placed the "scene" in British culture.*

OPPOSITE: *The difference is clear – Gordon's export gin is instantly distinguished from the green of its home sales product.*

A further sign of social acceptance was that, in the 1890s, distillers began to sell gin in bottles in response to the growing demand from the off licence trade. Until then gin was sold in barrels to the retailers who would bottle it themselves for customers to take home. With bottling came sophisticated labelling and advertising, all of which promoted gin as a quality product.

In 1898 there was a large-scale reorganization of the industry. Gordon's and Tanqueray joined forces to become the major presence in English distilling. Their combined economic power was enormous and, through rationalization of their production processes and the beginnings of a marketing strategy, they raised the status of gin as a sophisticated, international drink.

THE
MODERN
AGE

———————◆✦◆———————

By the beginning of the 20th century Dry Gin was beginning to
edge out the heavy, sweet Old Tom style. The main reason for
this was that it worked far better in the new craze for cocktails,
which had first arrived in Europe in the 1860s, brought over by
Americans who imported the fashion for sweet mixed drinks.

GIN IN VICTORIAN TIMES

Although cocktails seem to be the ultimate in modernity their origins are to be found in Victorian drinks such as cups, punches, flips and slings. American-style cocktails differed from these in that they were iced. The establishment of the Wenham Lake Ice Company in the Strand in 1845 made ice commercially available in London for the first time. The first American cocktail bar opened in the 1860s behind the Bank of England and soon cocktail bars popped up all over London. The Criterion in Piccadilly opened in 1870 and grand hotels like the Savoy and Claridge's boasted American Bars with a range of cocktails based on gin.

BELOW: *Gordon's takes on the cocktail.*

Some Londoners disapproved. In 1863, Henry Porter and George Roberts expressed their opinion in print: "for the sensation drinks which have lately travelled across the Atlantic we have no friendly feeling ... we will pass the American Bar ... and express our gratification at the slight success which 'Pick-me-up', and 'Corpse Reviver' have had in this country". However Mrs Isabella Beeton, the domestic goddess of Victorian England, was a fan and included recipes for Mint Juleps and Gin Slings in her famous 1861 edition of *The Book of Household Management*.

Jerry P. Thomas, aka the Professor, was one of the first and certainly the greatest of celebrity bartenders. Known as the "father of the American cocktail", by the time he was 33, he was earning more than the vice-president of the United States.

In 1862 he compiled *The Bar-Tender's Guide*. For the first time the oral tradition of the recipes of the first classic cocktails was committed to print. The 1876 edition included the first written recipe for the Tom Collins, whilst the 1887 revision had one of the first recorded recipes for the Martinez, a precursor of the Martini, made with Old Tom gin and sweet red vermouth. The

Professor toured Europe with his own portable bar giving demonstrations, and many European bartenders came to learn from the master.

For most of the 19th century drinkers in the United States stuck to Dutch-style genever and sweetened Old Tom and many cocktail books specified these in preference to Dry Gin. Until the 1890s imported Old Tom gin outsold Dry Gin but from then on Dry Gin slowly became the preferred cocktail spirit. This was because of the growing fashion for "dry" drinks such the Dry Martini, the Aviation and the Bronx where Dry Gin outshone the heavier, maltier styles.

ABOVE: *"Professor" Jerry Thomas was known for his showmanship and his signature drink, the Blue Blazer, involved setting whisky on fire and throwing it dramatically between two cocktail shakers.*

PROHIBITION IN AMERICA

On 17 January 1920, the Volstead Act passed through the US Congress and Prohibition came into force. It soon turned into a re-enactment of the 18th-century Gin Craze as millions of ordinary Americans overnight became amateur distillers and professional drinkers.

Organized crime quickly moved in on illicit alcohol manufacture and smuggling as there were vast profits to be made. An entire generation of Americans became criminals in one form or another, by either going to speakeasies, distilling at home or buying bootleg booze. Not exactly the scenario envisaged when many US towns closed down their jails on the eve of Prohibition in the anticipation that, once alcohol was banned, there would be no more crime. Bathtub gin was popular. It was a vile combination of industrial

RIGHT: *Never had being bad been so good – ironically, Prohibition in America produced a burgeoning drinking culture that was soon to cross the pond.*

alcohol, glycerine and juniper oil made in large containers to which water was added via the bath tap. To make it taste better, people added fruit juices, mixers and bitters – inventing a raft of new cocktails.

BELOW: *The effect of Prohibition on the export market was exactly the opposite of what the English distilleries had feared. Offshore sales boomed once private stocks ran out.*

English distillers had feared losing their most important export market as a result of Prohibition. In fact, the reputation of imported English gin reached new heights as, having experienced the effects of truly bad alcohol, Americans were ready to pay exorbitant sums for the "real McCoy" (reputedly named after a rum-runner operating in the Caribbean during Prohibition). It is estimated that, during Prohibition, London distilleries exported around 40 million dollars' worth of gin to the US via Canada, the West Indies and islands close to American shores. No questions were asked when requests came in that orders should be packaged so that they could float.

On 5 December 1933, the "noble experiment" of Prohibition ended, brought to a close largely by the very people who had been its most vociferous supporters. American mothers, weary of seeing their families criminalized and of the obscene profits made by gangsters like Al Capone and Dutch Schultz, led the charge to repeal the Act. Franklin D. Roosevelt had run for president on a platform that included ending Prohibition – and on the night he was elected, it is rumoured, mixed the first legal Martini in the White House for 13 years using Plymouth Gin.

America learned the hard way that drink was a part of civilized life and, like everything else in life, only the best was good enough. After Prohibition the demand for English gin soared in the US because the reputation of London Dry gin had never been higher. Brands like Gordon's and Gilbey's capitalized on this by building distilleries in the US. Tanqueray, who had donated US$1,000 to the anti-Prohibition movement, became the epitome of a well-made London dry style of gin in American eyes and exports went through the roof.

COCKTAILS AND THE JAZZ AGE

The 1920s and '30s were gin's glory days. The inter-war period was the age of glamour, an explosion of the new in technology, communications, fashion, the arts and popular culture. Along with fast cars, flappers in short skirts, cubist art, cinema and of course jazz, cocktails were the height of fashion.

RIGHT: *Cocktails as good as the name they bear ... Gordon's ensure their gin has its place at the heart of the new drinks craze.*

A traumatized generation who had survived the Great War simply wanted to have fun. This was a time when the old formal social order began to disappear. Dressing up for formal dinners had been abandoned and the cocktail hour was the perfect way to fill the vacuum. Cocktail parties became the rage, replacing the British custom of afternoon tea with early-evening cocktails. Reliable sources state that the cocktail party was introduced to London by an American-born hostess called Madame Alfredo de Pena in the late 1920s. Certainly from this time there is evidence of a growing cocktail culture influencing fashion, accessories, a host of gadgetry, literature, popular music and film. By now gin cocktails were simpler and new, sophisticated drinks such as the Clover Club and the White Lady were lapped up by high society.

The writer Evelyn Waugh portrayed the racy lives of young moneyed aristocrats and christened them the "Bright Young Things". Newspapers and magazines were fascinated by everything this smart set did – the first glimmerings of the modern obsession with celebrity. In his novel *Vile Bodies*

BELOW: *Gin became the perfect early-evening mellower for the fast set between the wars.*

Waugh describes the constant social whirl: "Masked parties, savage parties, Victorian parties, Greek parties, Russian parties, circus parties, parties where one had to dress as somebody else, almost naked parties in St John's Wood, parties in flats and studios and houses and ships and hotels and nightclubs, in windmills and swimming baths ... all the succession and repetition of massed humanity ... Those vile bodies." There was even a baby party with cocktails served in nursery mugs. And gin was the spur for this manic pace of life.

It was the same on the other side of the Atlantic despite Prohibition. There writers like F. Scott Fitzgerald chronicled the Roaring Twenties – a time when, as the *New York Times* put it, "gin was the national drink and sex the national obsession". Gin was Fitzgerald's favourite spirit – he believed no one could smell it on his breath – and the Gin Rickey was his favourite drink. One could easily imagine it being served at one of reputed bootlegger and mysterious millionaire Jay Gatsby's famous parties.

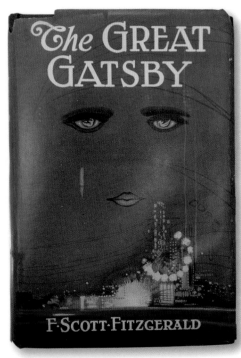

Riding the cocktail zeitgeist, distillers became much more sophisticated in their marketing. "Drinks never taste thin with Gordon's Gin" was the strapline for Gordon's advertising. At this time, Plymouth Gin and Booth's Gin were the two most famous gin brands in the world and both invested heavily in promoting their products.

Further down the social scale gin was "in", too. But cocktails never invaded the British pub, where the most popular mixers for gin were orange squash and ginger beer. A perennial favourite in working men's pubs was the Dog's Nose – a glass of gin poured into a pint of beer.

POST-WAR GIN BOOM

During the Second World War, all distilling from grain in Britain was prohibited in order to conserve stocks of grain for food, and most distilled alcohol was diverted to the war effort – described by the stoical British as "Cocktails for Hitler". However, despite strict rationing, some gin was still made for the domestic market using a molasses spirit. Once the war was over, English distillers were back in action, building huge export trades and re-establishing English-made gin as the world's most sophisticated spirit.

The popularity of gin reached its apogee in the 1950s and '60s, with Hollywood stars such as Errol Flynn and Humphrey Bogart rarely seen without a gin Martini in hand. Gin was glamorous: to this day the last take of every Hollywood movie is still called the "Martini shot" as that was the signal for everyone, from big-name star to the clapperboard guy, to celebrate in style.

Gin was sophisticated and the three-Martini lunch, which President Jimmy Carter was later to condemn, was standard fare in adland's Mad Men circles. David Embury's *The Fine Art of Mixing Drinks*, published in 1948, was a guide to making cocktails at home and it seemed as though few middle-class American households did not have their own cocktail bar where mixing a Martini was the evening ritual.

Gin remained the dominant white spirit right up until the late 1960s, a time when probably around half of any cocktail list would have been made up of gin-based drinks. Then came what seemed the unstoppable rise of vodka. By the 1970s, gin was almost stagnant in terms of growth. Many traditional brands simply disappeared. Others sat unloved on dusty shelves with no investment and no innovation. Even worse, gin lost its iconic image and was perceived as old-hat and old-fashioned.

After a while, though, it was all change again. The arrival of Bombay Sapphire with its classy packaging and less juniper-dominated taste profile had attracted a whole new audience for gin. And ultimately it inspired the launch of a new wave of innovative, unusually flavoured gins both from established brands and newcomers.

BELOW: *"Of all the gin joints in all the world she walks into mine" famously said Humphrey Bogart, the owner of Rick's bar in* Casablanca.

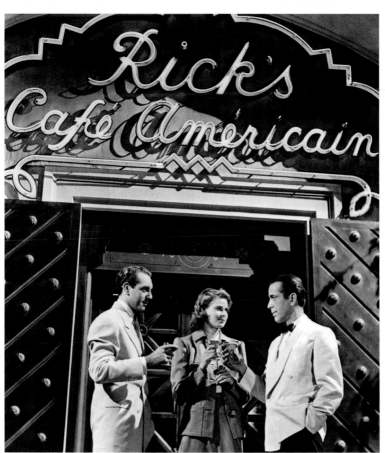

GIN IN THE 21ST CENTURY

By the year 2000 the renaissance of gin was well under way, its rebirth driven by a combination of factors. First the great revival of interest in classic, properly made cocktails that began in the 1990s. (Hard to believe now that not so long ago one could order a Martini in a relatively upmarket bar and be served a glass of red vermouth with a lump of ice!)

Since many of the iconic cocktails of the past are gin-based, influential and knowledgeable bartenders became passionate about gin. They spread the word as, similar to the fashion world where trends that start on the catwalk find their way to the High Street, innovations from high-end bars soon become mainstream. Fast forward to now and all over the world there are dedicated gin bars with over 100 gins on the barbacks and special Gin and Tonic menus featuring dozens of different ways to make a G and T not to mention dazzling cocktail lists featuring the old gin classics and new daring combinations. It's not really surprising: gin has always owed its success to its mixability.

Secondly the early 2000s saw a spate of interesting new gins like Hendrick's and Tanqueray 10 come to market inspired by the now obvious success of Bombay Sapphire. They not

BELOW: Tonic water is added to a glass of gin to create the most famous and glamorous of all cocktails, the Gin and Tonic.

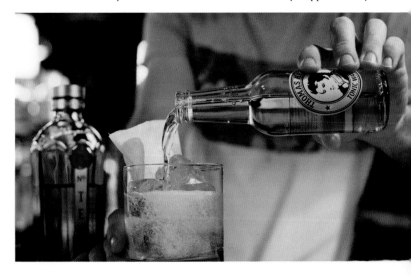

only revived interest in the category itself but also provided consumers with more real choice. Prior to that – and again it doesn't seem that long ago – you might have stood in the gin section of any off licence wondering whether to get a bottle of Gordon's, the more upmarket Beefeater or really lash out on that fancy new "blue" one i.e. Bombay Sapphire. And you would probably have been buying it for your Mum. Now every bottle shop, online retailer and even the supermarkets will have an almost bewildering array of gins to choose from.

But perhaps the most important factor that drives the current gin boom is to be found in the ongoing momentum of what has been described as "connoisseur consumerism". Consumers of all ages but especially in the younger demographic are willing to pay more for premium products but they want to know more about them too. The burgeoning of "foodie" culture had its corollary in drink. There's a quest for authenticity and heritage combined with many of the trends that have influenced modern gastronomy such as foraging for natural ingredients and using seasonal produce. Provenance is important in this and regionality plays a big part in consumer choices. With so many gins to choose from there's something very attractive about buying a gin that's distilled up the road at a local distillery from ingredients that

BELOW: Gin Master Classes at London-based distilleries, such as Hayman's, enthuse gin lovers.

grow wild all over one's own particular terroir. Technology has been crucial too and the success of many of the newer smaller gin brands is down to their ability to circumvent the old laborious routes to market using social media and online retailers to speak directly to a gin-loving audience.

The world has fallen in love with gin again. Modern gin-lovers not only have no shortage of choice for trying out their cocktail skills at home or discovering new flavour combinations in bars, they are also living in a golden age of gin. Production standards have never been higher and there's never been more genuine innovation. The astonishing boom in artisan-inspired distilling with small independent companies unafraid to push the boundaries has led to experimentation with new flavours and new methods of distillation whilst still respecting gin's heritage. Slowly but surely gin has finally regained its position as the queen of white spirits.

LEFT: *A glass Rotovap distilling device used by Porter's Gin in action.*

MAKING GIN

————◆◆◆◆◆————

At its most basic, gin is a clear, unaged alcohol, further distilled together with a selection of natural fruit and herb flavourings known as "the botanicals". Its neutral alcohol base in theory can be made out of any substance that will ferment. In practice the best gin is made from a grain spirit which is why you often see "100% Grain Spirit" prominently displayed on the label of a premium gin.

THE STYLES OF GIN

Following an EU directive of 2008 there are now legal definitions of the different styles of gin mostly designed to protect the tradition and craftsmanship attached to the London Dry style. This has given rise in turn to more rigorous definitions of "gin" and "distilled gin". This is how they work:

LONDON GIN: Does not have to be made in London, but must be made in a traditional still by re-distilling higher-quality than standard neutral alcohol (aka base spirit) with only natural flavourings (aka botanicals). No artificial flavourings can be added after distillation. Indeed, the only other substances that can be added after distillation are additional base spirit, water and a small amount of sweetening. London Gin cannot be coloured. Typical London Gins are Beefeater, Gordon's, Hayman's, Tanqueray and Whitley Neill.

DISTILLED GIN: Made in a traditional still by re-distilling neutral alcohol in the presence of natural flavourings. Additional natural or artificial flavourings may be added after distillation, as can other approved additives such as colouring. Typical distilled gins are new-wave gins like Hendrick's Gin, the London No. 1 Gin and Martin Miller's Gin.

GIN: Often known as "cold-compounded", it's made from any type of alcohol and does not have to be re-distilled; rather, the flavourings are simply added to the spirit. The flavourings can be artificial and additional sugar, colouring and other flavourings are also allowed. No real gin-lover is seriously interested in this type of gin, but it's useful to know why some bottles of supermarket gin cost half as much as a reputable brand.

These definitions can be confusing, as they are not based on how the gin tastes. Taste is highly subjective – which is why almost every official spirit definition is dictated by production methods.

BELOW: *The purity of gin is evident in both its crystal-clear appearance and aromatic taste.*

MAKING THE BASE SPIRIT

Distillation itself is a simple process that starts with a fermented liquor containing alcohol. Alcohol's boiling point is 78.3° C whilst water comes to the boil at 100° C. When fermented liquor is heated, therefore, the alcohol in it will separate and rise in vapour form. This vapour can then be run off, cooled and collected. As it cools, it returns to a liquid form – spirit, the *aqua vitae* of the ancients.

Neutral spirit, the base for gin, is made through a process of continuous distillation in a column still also known as a Coffey still after its creator, Aeneas Coffey, a Dublin excise officer. He may well have been the first to patent the still, in around 1830, but continuous stills seem to have been developed in other locations at around the same time.

There are many advantages to continuous distillation: a lighter, cleaner, more consistent spirit can be made in large quantities, and the final strength of the spirit can be accurately specified.

BELOW: *Continuous distillation at Greenall's.*

Most continuous stills consist of two linked columns – the analyser and the rectifier. Alcohol-bearing liquid in the form

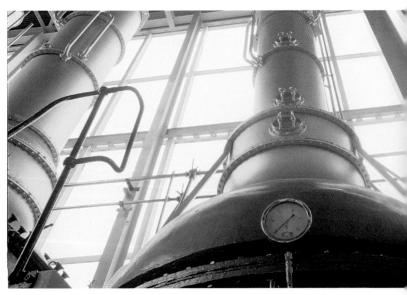

of a fermented wash is fed into the top of the rectifier. It runs down, via a pipe, to the bottom of the column and up to the top of the analyser, where it then starts to descend. Meanwhile steam enters the bottom of the analyser and rises slowly up through a series of horizontal perforated plates to heat the cool liquid. As the steam and liquid travel across the plates the alcohol, in vapour form, is separated out. It is then captured in a condenser where it cools and becomes liquid again.

The beauty of this system is that the distiller can collect the spirit at whatever strength he wants by adjusting the plates to capture the higher alcohols. Gin distillers require a neutral spirit at 96% ABV and that's exactly what they get.

Technically it would be easy enough to re-distil this on the spot but life is never that simple. Under British law, gin distillers are not allowed to produce their neutral spirit in the same location as the rectified spirit, ie gin – the result of an Act of 1825 intended to ensure unscrupulous distillers could no longer make sub-standard spirit for re-distillation into gin. So the spirit is transported to the gin distillery to be rectified or re-distilled.

Before the spirit is dispatched, samples are sent ahead for tasting. The spirit is tested again on arrival to ensure it conforms to the quality standards because, as any distiller will tell you, the spirit is the heart of a gin. Much depends on its quality and, equally, on its ability to maintain the consistency of the brand.

Given the octopus-like nature of large distilling concerns, most gin distillers source their grain spirit from sister companies within their own group of businesses. Gordon's and Tanqueray, for example, buy their spirit from a different part of Diageo's huge distilling complex in Cameronbridge, Scotland. The independent Greenwich Distillery also provides large quantities of neutral grain spirit for re-distillation.

THE SPICE TRADE

Gin is often described as "history in a glass". No wonder, when one considers the sheer diversity of berries, roots, peels, seeds and barks collectively known as "the botanicals" that are used to flavour gin.

And it's no coincidence that gin and its Dutch ancestor genever, both flavoured with juniper berries and other spices, are the national drinks of two great seafaring nations that once brought back all manner of exotica from the four corners of the world.

The trade in spices has been one of the most important shapers of European history, the cause of exploration, war and invasion for centuries. It could even be argued that the creation of great European colonial empires was mostly a by-product of the quest for domination of the spice trade, not its original purpose.

For millennia, the spice trade was controlled by Arab and north African middle-men who jealously protected the tortuous routes by which spices travelled from their places of origin in the East. They even invented such fantasies as the story that cassia grew in shallow lakes in China guarded by fierce winged animals! This sales pitch met with incredulity from the earliest times, with Pliny the Elder (23–79 AD) cynically commenting: "All these tales … have been evidently invented for the purpose of enhancing the price of these commodities."

In the 10th century, the powerful city-states Venice and Genoa prospered by importing spices directly from the Middle East and selling them at vast profit in Europe. A war between them, in 1398, saw Venice victorious and for the next hundred years the Venetian monopoly on trade routes was impossible to break. Towards the end of the 15th century, however, European navigational know-how developed dramatically and ships began to voyage further afield in the quest to reach spice-producing countries and trade directly with them. There were fortunes to be made, as nutmeg was more precious than gold and rent could be paid in peppercorns.

The Spanish royal house funded Christopher Columbus's quest to find a new route to the east by sailing west across the Atlantic in 1492. He discovered the New World but died believing he had reached China. Vasco Da Gama, the great Portuguese explorer and navigator, reached India by sailing around Africa in 1498, and set up trading posts that enabled Portugal to dominate trade with India for a century. In the early 1600s, the English and the Dutch established their own East India companies to build a network all over the Far East to trade in spices and other goods, often using brutal tactics. By the 17th century, the Dutch and the English pretty much controlled the spice trade: indeed it was often the cause of war between them. One such skirmish was resolved when England gave Holland the Banda Islands, where nutmeg grew, in return for a minor Dutch possession – Manhattan Island in the New World.

LEFT: *Navigator and explorer Vasco Da Gama opened up the trade route to India for Portugal at the end of the 15th century.*

THE BOTANICALS USED IN GIN

Botanicals make gin gin. And as soon as you walk into the room where the botanicals are stored in any distillery, you are instantly aware of how much of a debt today's drinks cabinets owe to yesterday's medicine chests. Almost all the botanicals used in gin originally had medicinal applications and many of them still do.

Each gin recipe has a different botanical mix and, whilst distillers may be prepared to talk about the botanicals they use, their actual proportions are never revealed. One can safely presume that most gins will contain juniper, coriander, angelica, citrus and orris. And, whilst there are reputedly over 120 botanical ingredients that can be used in gin, most gins confine themselves to seven or eight, rarely more than 12. There are of course exceptions: more of that in the *Brand Directory* on page 81.

On the next pages are the commonly found botanicals – starting with juniper, by law the principal flavouring in gin.

JUNIPER BERRIES

The juniper berries found in gin are a type of pine cone derived from *juniperus communis*, a small, coniferous shrub that grows wild throughout the northern hemisphere. Juniper gives gin its name and that instantly recognizable bittersweet taste of pine, lavender and camphor.

The medicinal applications of juniper go back to the dawn of civilization. The earliest recorded medicinal use of juniper berries occurs in an Egyptian papyrus dating back to around 1500 BC, in a recipe to cure tapeworm infestations. Juniper berries have also been found in Egyptian tombs as part of the embalming process.

BELOW: Botanical drawings of the flora of the juniper.

They were employed by both the Greeks and the Egyptians to ward off infections and this evolved into a belief, common throughout the Middle Ages, that the vapours from juniper berries could prevent leprosy and the bubonic plague. When the Black Death, a virulent form of bubonic plague, stalked Europe in the 14th century, killing more than one-third of the population, people even wore masks filled with juniper, breathing in its aromas to protect them from the deadly disease. Strangely this practice might actually have had some effect as juniper oil is still used in veterinary medicine to prevent fleas, and it was fleas carried by black rats that spread the bubonic plague. For humans, oil of juniper was given to alleviate kidney and bladder infections and also to treat indigestion and other digestive disorders.

The juniper used in gin is carefully sourced with the best growing wild on hillsides in Italy and Macedonia. The berries take two to three years to mature and are harvested in the autumn of their second year by beating the branches of the shrubs with sticks so that only the blue berries fall into baskets below, leaving the green ones to ripen further. After harvest the berries are spread out to dry. Once mature they develop their familiar blackish colour and are rich in aromatic oil. Because each year's crop will be slightly different, distillers regularly test a number of samples to create the exact blend of berries they require.

ALMONDS

Almond trees grow all over southern Europe. An important item of trade in the Middle Ages, almond oil is still used in medicines and skin care preparations. The bitter almond, not the sweet, is used in gin. It's also the source of prussic acid aka cyanide. First ground to release their rich oil, almonds impart a marzipan-like sweetness and softness to gin's complexity.

ANGELICA ROOT

In European folk medicine angelica has been viewed as a magical herb for over a thousand years. People made necklaces from angelica leaves to protect their children from illness and witchcraft whilst the root was believed to protect against plague. Indeed the plant takes its name from the Greek word *arkhangelos* (archangel) because of the tradition that the archangel Michael appeared in a dream to tell of its effectiveness against the bubonic plague and other infectious diseases. In Chinese medicine angelica is known as *dong quai* and prescribed for a wide variety of ailments.

Almost all gin recipes will include shredded angelica root as not only does it make Dry Gin dry, it has woody, earthy notes that help to create an integrated botanicals profile.

ANGELICA SEED

Angelica seeds are widely used in traditional folk and Chinese medicines and are also found in many liqueurs that started life as herbal remedies. In gin, their fragrant, slightly musky notes complement the taste of juniper. Distillers in the past sometimes substituted angelica seeds for juniper when the latter was hard to source, particularly because angelica grows wild throughout the UK.

ABOVE: *Angelica root was indigenous to the very northern parts of Europe, but it is now found across the continent.*

BERGAMOT PEEL

Bergamot is a citrus fruit closely related to the orange but much more sour and thus rarely grown for its juice. Instead the juice of bergamot is often used in Italian indigenous medicine to treat malaria and its essential oil is popular in aromatherapy. In the 18th century, oil of bergamot was used to flavour snuff, gin and, of course, the famous Earl Grey tea, so there is provenance here. Bergamot's instantly recognizable musky, perfumed aromas are now found in a number of relatively new gins.

CARAWAY SEEDS

A member of the parsley family, caraway is native to Europe, Asia, and north Africa but is now widely cultivated throughout the world. Caraway has been used in medicine for centuries. The Egyptians first recommended it as a digestive aid in about 1500 BC and it is still used in babies' gripe water. Caraway is also a common cooking ingredient in Germanic countries where it is used to flavour rye bread and liqueurs such as Kummel. In the still it releases sweet musk aromas not unlike liquorice.

CARDAMOM PODS

The word itself sums up the exoticism of the Far East and, after saffron and vanilla, cardamom is the third most expensive spice in the world. Cardamom originally grew wild in the rainforests of the Western Ghats in India. In the 19th century British colonists established cardamom as a secondary crop on coffee plantations in other parts of the subcontinent. To this day extracts of cardamom seeds are used to treat skin conditions and to aid digestion in south Asia.

Before they enter the still as part of the botanical recipe, cardamom pods are crushed to allow the full flavour of the little black seeds inside to emerge. Cardamom brings warm, spicy, aromatic flavours to gin.

CASSIA BARK

Cassia oil derives from the bark of cinnamon-like trees that grow in the tropics and is also known as bastard cinnamon or Chinese cinnamon.

It resembles cinnamon in flavour but is stronger and more bitter. In China cassia is considered one of the six great spices. In the West it is often used in skin care and cassia extracts used to be mixed with almond oil to make Macassar oil – a popular Victorian hair oil for men which produced an urgent requirement for anti-macassars, those little white squares of crocheted fabric that your great-aunt draped over the backs of her chairs. Cassia smells and tastes very like Dentyne chewing gum – sharp and pungent, almost medicinal.

CHAMOMILE

In Ancient Egypt chamomile was dedicated to the gods and its name comes from the Greek for "ground apple" due to its distinctive scent. In Spain chamomile is called *Manzanilla*, meaning little apple. It's also the name of a light Spanish sherry, either because chamomile may once have been used to flavour it or because the sherry is reminiscent of its aroma. In Anglo-Saxon times chamomile was used widely in beer-making until hops took over. In the Middle Ages, it was a "strewing" herb, spread on floors to make rooms smell sweeter. Chamomile is still a favourite garden herb and is used in herbal infusions and aromatherapy for its soothing and calming properties.

CINNAMON BARK

Another word that conjures up images of faraway tropical places, cinnamon is the bark of the cinnamon tree commonly found in Sri Lanka. It is used in many different types of cuisine and also in incense, massage oils and in ancient times to cure snakebites, freckles, the common cold, and kidney troubles. As in cooking, a pinch goes a long way in gin distillation as its warm, aromatic flavours can overpower.

CORIANDER SEED

BELOW: Coriander seeds have been used as a spice for more than 5,000 years and their oils as a medicine since the days of Hippocrates.

Coriander seed is one of the oldest spices in recorded history, with evidence of its use dating to over 5,000 years ago. Indeed coriander has been cultivated around the Mediterranean since ancient Egyptian times and coriander seeds were found in tombs of the 21st Dynasty. Hippocrates, the father of medicine, first promoted its use as a medicine because its essential oil has many therapeutic properties. It's often used to cure conditions such as rheumatism, colic and neuralgia.

Coriander seeds are the second most commonly used botanical in gin and have formed part of the botanicals mix for centuries. If coriander seems an exotic ingredient for 18th-century English distillers, it should be remembered that coriander was grown commercially in southern England long before the days of global warming.

Coriander seeds look like mini-rugby balls and have a fresh, slightly spicy, sage and lemon flavour. Most distillers source their coriander from southern Europe although spicier gins like Bombay Dry and Bombay Sapphire use the more pungent coriander from Morocco.

CUBEB BERRIES

Cubeb berries are the fruit of the cubeb plant, a cardamom-like tropical vine that is a member of the pepper family. It has small white flowers that develop into tiny reddish-brown seeds or berries. Cubeb is native to Indonesia and first came to Europe via Venetian trade with the Arabs. It was once used in herbal remedies and was believed to have aphrodisiac qualities. It became a popular substitute for the vastly more expensive black pepper in the Middle Ages.

ELDERFLOWER

Elder trees are common throughout Europe and grow wild in northern temperate regions. In folklore the elder tree is a symbol of grief because the Crucifixion cross was made from its wood. It was also believed to be the tree from which Judas hanged himself. The elder has magical associations throughout Europe: it is widely believed that burning elder wood brings bad luck but that elder sprigs hung inside provide protection from witches.

Both elderflowers and elderberries are used to make wines and cordials. Elderflower has a complex and distinctive sweet smell and imparts fresh, herbal, floral notes with an acrid fruity undertone. Some describe this as the aroma of white grapes, others as cat's pee.

GINGER

Ginger is the rhizome of *zingiber officinale* and is also found in either root or powder form in many different types of cuisine. Ginger is a staple of Chinese traditional medicine and was mentioned in the writings of Confucius. It was also one of the earliest spices known in western Europe. Modern-day ginger ale and ginger beer have evolved from tavern keepers' 19th-century custom of leaving out small containers of ground ginger for people to sprinkle into their beer. In gin it imparts dry spicy flavours.

LEMON PEEL

Medicinally prized for its high vitamin C content, lemon juice was once given daily to sailors serving on Royal Navy ships to prevent scurvy. In gin, dried lemon peel – like other citrus fruit such as orange, lime and grapefruit – adds a crisp, sharp bite that enhances the juniper flavour. Some gins have a stronger citrus profile than others, particularly more traditional gins. But it's rare to find one that does not include citrus in some form.

LIQUORICE

Liquorice is grown for its long taproots, a source of natural sweetness with many medicinal qualities. It is widely used in the treatment of bronchitis and is also a common ingredient in cough medicines. Gin distillers often source their liquorice from China. It contains sugar, bitter compounds, and a substance that produces a distinctive woody, sweet flavour. Liquorice also softens and rounds out gin's mouthfeel.

MEADOWSWEET

Meadowsweet is a perennial herb that grows profusely throughout Europe, the eastern US and Canada. It has sweet-smelling white flowers and slightly almond-smelling leaves and was one of the three herbs considered to be sacred by the Druids. It's mentioned in Chaucer's *Knight's Tale* as an ingredient of a drink called "Save". In Elizabethan times meadowsweet flowers were added to herb beers and wines, and the leaves were placed into claret cups. It was also a popular strewing herb.

Meadowsweet is an excellent digestive remedy. Importantly it's also a source of salicylic acid, the basis of aspirin, the modern-day wonder drug whose name is derived from the old botanical name for meadowsweet – *spiraea ulmaria*. Meadowsweet's herbal, sweet, floral character enhances the freshness and zestiness of gin.

ORANGE PEEL

Dried orange peel is a crucial element of the botanical recipe and generally bitter or Seville orange is used rather than the sweet orange as its oil is more pungent. Bitter orange oil is also used in foods, cosmetics, and aromatherapy products. In gin it imparts fresh clean citrus notes that provide a counterbalance to the more pungent botanicals.

ABOVE: *Dried orange peel is a key botanical ingredient in gin, but it has numerous other uses in medicine and orange oil is popular with aromatherapists.*

ORRIS ROOT

Orris is the rhizome of *iris fiorentina*, dried and ground to a fine powder. Many famous perfumes like Chanel No. 5 have orris root as their base note and it is also found in talcum powder and potpourri mixes as well as in the delicate spice mix – *ras-el-hanout* – used in Middle Eastern cooking.

Orris is commercially grown in Italy. At harvest time plants of at least three years old are dug up with a long-handled hoe. The rhizomes or roots are carefully broken off, and then peeled by hand. The peeled orris is scrubbed in water and left to dry on wire racks. At this stage orris is virtually odourless. It is stored for at least two years in order for it to develop its distinctive aromas. Then it is ground into a fine powder.

Aromatic and floral in itself with a hint of Parma violet, in gin as in perfume, orris acts as a miracle fixing agent, holding the volatile elements of the other aromatics together.

RE-DISTILLING THE BOTANICALS

Making premium gin is a craft and distillers all have their own ways of doing things, according to their own traditions and how they want their gin to taste. One major point of difference is between the "one-shot method" and the "two-shot method".

THE ONE-SHOT METHOD

Using the one-shot method the distillation process starts with charging copper pot stills with neutral grain spirit, water and the botanicals in the exact proportions of the recipe. The mix is then distilled and finally water is added to reduce it to bottling strength.

THE TWO-SHOT METHOD

Gordon's, Tanqueray and many other gins are made by the two-shot method where the still is charged with botanicals at several times the strength of the recipe. After distillation, neutral alcohol is added to restore the original proportions of the recipe. The advantage of course is that twice the amount of gin can be made in a single distillation.

STEEPING THE BOTANICALS

Some distillers steep the botanical mix in the still before distillation for anything from 24 hours up to several days. It's more time-consuming and, because the stills can't be run during this time, more expensive but they believe it results in a fuller extraction of flavour from the botanicals. Others don't steep because they believe the botanicals become stewed. I defy anyone to spot which gins have been steeped and which not by tasting the final result, so the decision is really part of each brand's unique history and production.

THE STILLS

Most gin stills are onion-shaped copper pot stills exactly the same as the ones used to make malt whisky. They have elongated "swan" necks to extract the more fragrant, more volatile elements of the spirit and each will have a condenser beside it to cool the alcohol-bearing vapour back to liquid.

Copper is used in pot stills because it has the ability to remove sulphury or vegetable aromas by chemical reaction. The shape of the pot still also affects flavour, as it controls the speed at which the spirit vaporizes and begins to embed the botanical aromas. Distillers don't like to change a winning formula so, when one of the stills at the Diageo distillery (where Gordon's and Tanqueray are made) had to be replaced, the still-makers

ABOVE: *A specially adapted Carterhead still used in the now rare "racking" method of distillation.*

were instructed to copy the original precisely – even down to replicating dents and bashes. At the Black Friars Distillery in Plymouth, the 160-year-old still has a shorter neck than normal and a steeper curve in the lyne pipe. Why? Because that's the way it's always been, and because Master Distiller Sean Harrison believes that this design contributes to his gin's full-bodied character.

The other main type of still is the Carterhead, developed in the 19th century by the two Carter brothers who were originally employed by the renowned Aeneas Coffey. The Carterhead uses the vapour infusion method, once called "racking" – see above.

BATCH DISTILLATION

The batch distillation process starts with charging the copper pot still with the botanicals and spirit usually reduced to a strength of about 45% ABV with water. Some distillers steep the botanical mix in the still before distillation, some don't – see above. The still is gently heated to around 70 to 80 degrees C. Remember alcohol boils at 78.3 and, when this temperature is reached, the botanical-infused spirit begins to rise as a vapour and hits the onion-shaped part of the still. At this point the onion part of the still is relatively cool so the vapour condenses and falls back into the still. This is called reflux and happens repeatedly until the onion has heated up sufficiently to allow the spirit to pass through as a vapour and cross over the high swan neck of the still.

A distillation usually takes between seven and eight hours from start to finish. It's a mysterious process, with each botanical releasing its flavour at different point in the cycle. Citrus elements emerge first, then juniper and coriander, followed by rooty botanicals such as orris, angelica and liquorice. They combine to create a glorious mélange of aromas that fill the stillroom.

The speed at which the still is run is crucial. Too fast and all the flavours bundle up and cross over together in a rush. Too slow and undesirable elements of the spirit are picked up. To control the rate at which the spirit boils and captures the botanical flavours, the flow of steam can be turned up or down much like controlling the heat under a boiling pot.

Once the flavours of the botanicals are firmly embedded, the vapour becomes liquid again. It's pumped into copper tubing surrounded by cool water inside the condenser next to the still. As the botanical-infused vapour travels down this column, it is cooled and returns to a liquid form.

During distillation the first part of the liquid, the foreshots or "heads" sometimes as much as the first 20 litres through the still, is discarded because it contains unwanted flavours – oily or off, too strong, too weak.

About halfway through each run the feints or "tails" will start to emerge and when they deteriorate into unacceptable "stewed" flavours they too are diverted. (Very often the foreshots and feints are sold to make industrial alcohol products such as antifreeze or solvents or they are kept to be re-distilled later.)

Deciding when to make the "middle cut" as it is called is probably a distiller's most important job and a crucial part of the recipe. In some of the bigger distilleries it's often done by gently humming computers but in smaller distilleries it is almost always done in real time by a real person who will taste the liquid coming through the spirit safe until it has the characteristics of the original recipe. Some distilleries even run yearly checks to make sure that the noses of the stillroom staff are picking up the right flavours.

ABOVE: *Master Distiller Sean Harrison believes that the shorter neck of the still at the Black Friars Distillery contributes to the full-bodied character of Plymouth Gin.*

ABOVE: *Beefeater's Master Distiller Desmond Payne breathes in the aroma before tasting the gin.*

OPPOSITE: *The glasshouses at Bombay Sapphire where the botanicals are grown.*

The heart of the gin is diverted into the spirit receiver here at about 80–85% ABV. No two distillers will cut at exactly the same time or at exactly the same strength. That decision remains a trade secret. Some gins however are noticeably heavier with more robust aromas. This is partly because they contain larger proportions of rooty substances and partly one supposes because they will have been left to run longer to pick up the heavier elements of the spirit. Others are lighter in taste with more pronounced citric tones and will probably have been cut at an earlier point in the run.

Most gins are then "rested" in large metal containers. At this stage the gin then goes through another quality control tasting and may also be analysed by gas chromatography to ensure product quality and consistency.

The other main method of distillation is by vapour infusion. Here the botanicals are carefully layered in a copper basket at the very top of a Carterhead still, i.e. a pot still with a long rectifying column on top. Neutral grain alcohol and water are put into the still that is then heated. When the spirit meets the botanicals it is in vapour form and it passes slowly through the baskets, embedding the different flavours before it returns to liquid. The effect is one of "steaming" rather than the more traditional "boiling" process. Vapour infusion is used to produce all the gins in the Bombay family.

BOTTLING STRENGTH

Once distillation is complete, the gin is reduced to its bottling strength by adding water. In European law the alcoholic content of all gin must be at least 37.5% ABV (equivalent to 75 proof in North America). Most experts agree that for a gin to be considered premium it should be bottled at at least 40% ABV. Why, you may ask, when the gin will be served with a mixer or in a cocktail and so diluted considerably? Does it really matter? Yes, because alcohol carries the complex flavours of the botanicals. Below 40% ABV some of the more volatile citrus elements and aromatic top notes in gin are lost.

A word too about water. It is no accident that the 18th-century distillers made sure that their distilleries were

BELOW: A Gordon's bottling factory. Once distillation is complete, gin is diluted back to a drinkable strength before it is packaged for sale.

located in those parts of London noted for the purity of their water. Water accounts for an alarmingly high proportion of a bottle of gin and the water used in the distilling process and to reduce the final spirit must be exceptionally pure.

Because gin is made from wholly natural ingredients and is unaged, it contains very few of the organic chemicals known collectively as "congeners". Congeners are technically impurities but they contribute greatly to flavour. For example, over 400 different congeners have been identified in some malt whiskies. Gin generally has an average of three congeners. Research has shown that hangovers are related to the quantity of congeners in alcohol and so gin is the least likely drink to produce that dreaded morning-after feeling. That's good to know.

BRAND DIRECTORY

This Brand Directory is divided into two parts; this first section covers well-loved and well-known gins, the backbone of the industry, who have been stalwarts of the gin world long before gin became cool again. With very few exceptions they are all premium gins, bottled at above 40% ABV. Or they are historic brands with an interesting story.

Although UK-made gins dominate this Directory, the best US, French and Spanish gins are also included wherever possible. All are widely available either in retail or online.

For reasons of space, the specific botanicals mentioned throughout the Directory are the ones that differentiate each brand's own recipe so, unless stated, assume that each gin will contain the essential botanical DNA – juniper, coriander, citrus, orris root and angelica.

AVIATION

Aviation Gin is typical of the style of gin emerging from small American craft distilleries. Made with the Aviation cocktail in mind, it has juniper, cardamom, coriander, lavender, anise seed, sarsaparilla, and dried orange peel. Re-distilled with a 100% rye-grain neutral spirit and bottled at 42% ABV, it also has strong hints of Dutch *jonge genever*. Aviation is the ideal base for the many citrus-based vintage gin cocktails that are back in fashion again.

BEEFEATER LONDON DRY

Beefeater is the quintessential English gin created by James Burrough, a Victorian entrepreneur who had trained as a pharmacist. In 1863 he returned to London and purchased the Chelsea distilling firm of John Taylor for £400.

When the *phylloxera* blight struck European vineyards, brandy, the base spirit for many of his liqueurs, became difficult to obtain and expensive. James began to focus on gin and constantly experimented to find the perfect recipe. Today Beefeater is very much the gin that James Burrough created – a clean, bold gin with a strong juniper character and distinctive bitter orange notes. Other botanicals in the mix are almond, angelica seed and liquorice. They are steeped in a pure grain spirit for 24 hours, then run through a copper pot still. The final spirit is reduced to 40% ABV.

Beefeater is the only major international brand of London Dry Gin that is still actually made in London – in Kennington, within sight of the famous Oval cricket ground. Beefeater has long had a major export trade thanks to its clever positioning in the 1950s as a characteristically "English", not to say London, product and the use of the iconic image of the Beefeaters, the traditional warders of the Tower of London. That tradition continues and Beefeater is the gin of London as well as a leading brand found on back bars all over the world. A new visitor centre at the Kennington Distillery is now a must-go destination for gin fans. (*See Gin Places* on page 190 for details.)

Master distiller Desmond Payne celebrated 50 years in the gin industry in 2017 and has overseen many limited-edition additions to the core Beefeater portfolio such as the new Beefeater Pink made with fresh strawberries that are added post-distillation.

BEEFEATER 24

Beefeater 24 is a super luxury addition to the Beefeater Gin family and is almost unique in incorporating leaf teas into the botanical recipe. So the core Beefeater recipe is taken to another level with the addition of a blend of Chinese green and rare Japanese Sencha teas plus grapefruit peel. On the nose, notes of citrus, juniper and the aromatic scent of Sencha are immediately apparent. In the mouth, there's a burst of citrus followed by juniper, developing into a long finish with spicy coriander. Bottled at 45% ABV, its complex flavour profile has inspired a host of new gin drinks such as The MarTEAini (*see* page 187).

BERKELEY SQUARE

Berkeley Square is a premium gin from Warrington-based G & J Greenall that is inspired by the herbs of an English physic garden – hence the addition of basil, sage, lavender and kaffir lime leaves. It is made using an unusual technique. First, the core botanicals and the kaffir lime leaves are left to steep in the spirit for a day alongside the other botanicals, which are wrapped in muslin. Then the still is run very slowly to capture the delicate essential oils of the bouquet garni. The green herbaceous botanicals in Berkeley Square make it an ideal gin to experiment with for interesting herbal cocktails, with garnishes like cucumber and basil.

BLOOM GIN

Another Warrington gin, Bloom is based on a triple-distilled pure grain spirit re-distilled with honeysuckle, pomelo and chamomile as well as the more "standard" botanicals. The result is a very fragrant, floral gin with an aromatic sweetness like candied fruit. The essential oils of pomelo (a close relative of grapefruit) impart a zingy citrus freshness. Ideal for a summer G and T garnished with a grapefruit slice.

BLUECOAT GIN

Named for the blue uniforms of the American militia in the Revolution, this American Dry Gin hails from Philadelphia. It prides itself on using certified organic botanicals that are re-distilled in a neutral grain spirit made from rye, wheat, barley and corn, then filtered before bottling at 47% ABV. Batch-distilled over a slow 10-hour process, the resulting liquid is exceptionally smooth, with juniper and citrus notes and faint aromas of rosehip and grapefruit.

The Bombay Spirits Company was established in the early 1960s by Allan Subin, a New York-based lawyer-turned-importer of premium-quality spirits. He saw the opportunity to create a new, very British gin to challenge Tanqueray and Beefeater in the United States, and approached the Greenall's distillery with a name and a marketing plan, but without a specific taste. Greenall's came up with Bombay Original Dry based on a gin recipe found in their archives dating back to the 1760s. Made from a 100% pure grain spirit and bottled at 37.5% ABV, it's a London Dry Gin that uses eight botanicals – the traditional ones plus almonds, liquorice and cassia bark. It's distilled by vapour infusion in a Carterhead still (*see* page 73).

On the nose juniper, coriander and liquorice dominate. The taste is full-bodied, with piney juniper, lemon citrus

and warm spice. The mighty Bacardi Martini now owns all the Bombay brands and has reintroduced Bombay Original to the UK and other European territories. Recently they have reduced the alcoholic strength to 37.5% ABV in a head-to-head tussle with Gordon's.

From a gin-lover's point of view a far better decision was to build a state-of-the-art distillery and Visitor Centre in Laverstoke, Hampshire where all the gins in the Bombay family are now made. This is a genuinely awe-inspiring investment that offers quite possibly the best distillery visitor experience in the world (*see Gin Places* on page 190 for details).

BOMBAY SAPPHIRE

Bombay Sapphire is the gin that gently led the gin category out of its slump. Developed in the 1980s by Michel Roux, the driving force behind Absolut vodka, it's an immensely stylish premium gin that has attracted a whole new audience of gin-drinkers.

Michel Roux worked closely with Ian Hamilton, Greenall's head distiller at the time, to perfect the new gin, using Bombay Original Dry as the starting point. They experimented with many botanicals, test-distilling each to measure their effect on the recipe. Eventually two exotic varieties of pepper, Grains of Paradise and Cubeb Berries, were chosen. Their addition produced a gin with greater liveliness, adding unusual floral pepper and spice notes. The interaction of these two new botanicals with the others in the recipe during distillation differentiated Bombay Sapphire from the original Bombay, giving a bright juniper taste with exotic peppers on the finish. No other botanicals were added or taken away.

Bombay Sapphire is also made in a Carterhead still through infusion to pick up these more subtle spicy and fragrant aromas. Stylish packaging and a distinctive blue bottle referencing the glory days of the Raj and the famous Star of Bombay – a stunning sapphire discovered in Sri Lanka – make Bombay Sapphire instantly recognizable on every back bar. Perhaps the biggest favour Bombay Sapphire did for gin, however, is that it was the first brand to actually talk about what's inside the bottle. That alone got both bartenders and gin-lovers talking about the juniper spirit, and its success encouraged other gin distillers to experiment with innovative ingredients.

Bombay Sapphire tends to be more laid-back than many other London Dry Gins. On tasting it's slightly sweet on the nose with delicate juniper, spice and citrus flavours following on. Fresh and clean with an elegant finish, Bombay Sapphire is a barkeep's dream with extraordinary versatility in long drinks and cocktails. Speciality Sapphire serves include the Bombay and Cran and the Wet Martini where the extra vermouth enhances Sapphire's floral and spice flavours.

BOMBAY SAPPHIRE EAST

Bombay Sapphire East adds Thai lemongrass and Vietnamese black peppercorns to the Bombay Sapphire botanical recipe. It delivers a lovely big pepper hit alongside fragrant spice and a citrus sweetness. Bombay Sapphire East has been created with the G and T in mind, and these spicy, earthy flavours more than hold their own against even the sweetest of American-style tonic water.

BOODLES GIN

Although nowadays it is more often found at the other side of the Atlantic, Boodles is a traditional British brand dating back to 1847. It is bottled in the States at 45% ABV proof and is a high-strength, very dry gin with citrus and spice notes.

BOOTH'S GIN

Although the Booth's brand is drastically devalued nowadays and is only made in the US under licence, the name still has the power to stir the blood of gin aficionados. Word is that bottles of original Booth's High & Dry change hands on eBay for ridiculous amounts. Not surprising really when one considers that Booth's can make a good claim to be the oldest surviving London Gin in the world. In its heyday it was constantly raved about by leading drinks writers – for example, recommended as the only gin for a Pink Gin by the great, heroic drinker Kingsley Amis.

The first recorded evidence of the firm of Booth's is a document of 1569 that mentions the Booth family as wine merchants. Presumably they expanded into gin distilling as many wine merchants did, although there is no official record until the listing of Philip Booth & Company Distillers in Clerkenwell in the 1778 *Directory of Merchants*.

In 1819 Philip's son, Felix Booth, inherited the business and began to transform Booth's into the largest distiller in the country. In 1829 Felix sponsored Captain John Ross's expedition to map the fabled North West Passage. Although that remained elusive, the expedition discovered the true position of the magnetic North Pole and Ross mapped much of the area, naming huge swathes of it after his patron. Hence one rather bizarrely finds Boothia Peninsula, Felix Harbour, Cape Felix and the Gulf of Boothia in the extreme north of Canada. Felix was also instrumental in opening up the export trade for gin.

Booth's made several London Dry-style gins. Booth's Finest was unique at the time in that it had a slightly golden colour, originally because it had been stored by accident in sherry casks. The resultant ageing improved its taste so much that it was henceforth always "rested" in sherry casks. Sadly at the time the fashion was for clear gin as that signified purity so its reputation suffered. How times change; if Booth's Finest was around today it would be hailed as an innovative breakthrough in new styles of gin. (*See Aged Gins* on page 164.)

BELOW: *The Royal seal of approval was a great selling point for Booth's Finest Old Dry Gin.*

To promote its gins Booth's commissioned *An Anthology of Cocktails* in the 1930s, which featured the cocktail choices and photographs of well-known characters such as entertainer and heartthrob Ivor Novello. One of the first known examples of celebrity endorsement in advertising, it was extremely popular and original copies are now collector's items.

After World War II Booth's High & Dry, developed specifically for cocktails, was targeted at the American market. It never quite cracked it and Booth's gins began to be passed around the great distilling conglomerates, ending up in the hands of Diageo who still own the rights.

BOUDIER SAFFRON GIN

Saffron Gin, made by Gabriel Boudier of Dijon, is a direct link to the gin-distilling history of northern France, which, as a former part of the Low Countries, was once a genever hub. Based on an old colonial recipe, Saffron Gin is rich in the exotic botanicals that were the fashion at that time – iris, fennel and of course, saffron. Saffron imparts a rich orange colour whilst a distinctive spiciness comes from fennel and angelica seed. Think of it as an alternative to Aperol, the Italian liqueur that has gained enormously in popularity of late, and serve either with tonic and a slice of orange or topped up with Cava or Prosecco for a perfect aperitif.

BROKER'S GIN

Broker's Gin makes much of its English heritage with its bowler hat and city gent pinstripe packaging. It's distilled in a copper pot still at the Langley Distillery near Birmingham. The botanical mix, which includes cassia bark, cinnamon, liquorice and nutmeg, is steeped in neutral grain spirit made from 100% English wheat before distilling. The result is a very London-style gin with a rich aromatic nose. Spirits guru F. Paul Pacult summed up the taste experience: "In the mouth it sits well on the tongue and, thankfully, is the proper level of alcohol for gin, 94 proof (47% ABV). It finishes long, semi-sweet, tangy and luscious. A superbly made London Dry Gin that deserves a very close look by any admirer of that style."

BULLDOG GIN

Another very classic London Gin distilled in London and made from 100% British grain, Bulldog is triple-filtered for extra smoothness. Its makers have sought out the unusual and the exotic in terms of flavour, so botanicals include such eccentricities as lotus leaves, lavender, poppy and the reputedly aphrodisiac Dragon Eye, a cousin of the lychee fruit. Big, intense flavours, a good solid 40% ABV strength and lots of aromatic spice make this one for a Martini – especially the Dirty version with olive juice.

BURNETT'S WHITE SATIN

Burnett's White Satin is a venerable English brand that was established by Robert Burnett in the late 18th century. He acquired a huge distillery in Vauxhall that had been built in 1767 by Sir Joseph Mawbey. It was then the biggest in London and contemporary reports record that there were seldom fewer than 2,000 hogs constantly grunting, and kept entirely on the grains. (A common practice of distillers at the time was to keep pigs and feed them on the waste from distilling – very eco.) Robert Burnett became Sheriff of London in 1794 and was knighted the following year.

Burnett's White Satin is another classic English brand that has had its ups and downs. For years, it was one of the biggest-selling gins in the UK but then it became a cheap compounded gin made with a molasses spirit and artificial flavourings. It has now, however, regained its place as a traditionally distilled proper London Dry Gin at 40% ABV. Pleasantly junipery with warm spicy flavours, it's an everyday gin that is a very good alternative to domestic Gordon's for those who still smart at the latter's reduction in alcoholic strength.

CADENHEAD'S OLD RAJ

Cadenhead's Old Raj gin is technically neither a London nor a Distilled Gin and is made by cold compounding. So why is it included here, you might ask? Because, despite this, it's a very good gin, most likely because it uses natural, not artificial flavourings and it has an exceptionally high alcoholic strength. It's made by macerating each botanical in a mixture of alcohol and water, then distilling them separately in a small pot still. The resulting infusions are combined with a neutral grain spirit and saffron is added for colouring. At 46% ABV, it is spirity and peppery with a slight medicinal taste, at 55% ABV it is very aromatic and rounded.

CAORUNN GIN

Scottish whisky distillers have been at the forefront of the great gin revival. It's not surprising – they have the stills, the spirit and generations of distilling expertise. Caorunn (pronounced "ka-roon") Gin is small batch gin made in Scotland by Inver House Distillers, the malt whisky experts who own Balmenach Distillery on Speyside.

Caorunn is Gaelic for the rowanberry and the gin includes rowanberries and a further 10 botanicals including some unusual, particularly Scottish ingredients – such as Coul Blush apple, heather, bog myrtle and dandelion – that grow in or near the distillery itself. It is made by a unique vapour infusion method whereby neutral grain spirit is heated to vapour in a special still called a copper berry chamber, made in the 1920s. The chamber is round and contains four large trays on which the botanicals are placed. As the vapour passes through the trays it picks up the flavours of the botanicals in a long slow process. When it cools and returns to liquid the botanicals are firmly embedded in the spirit.

Reduced to a bottling strength of 41.8% ABV, Caorunn is a real taste experience. On the nose it's juniper with fruity notes of rowan and apple that develop into a clean, crisp, aromatic flavour with a pronounced fruitiness and slight heather honey sweetness. A long dry finish makes this one for those who are fans of mellow gins. Try it in a Summer Gin Punch or as its signature serve with tonic water and a slice of red apple for garnish.

CITADELLE GIN

Another French gin, Citadelle is made in Ars by renowned distillers Gabriel & Andreu. It's based on an original 18th-century recipe from the former Citadelle Distillery in Dunkirk and is typical of French gins in that it is highly flavoursome and aromatic with rare botanicals such as savory, fennel, violets and star anise. Bottled at 44% ABV, the use of so many botanicals can somewhat overpower its juniper character but unusual herbal notes and a pleasantly perfumed palate more than make up for this.

CITY OF LONDON DRY GIN

City of London Dry Gin (or COLD Gin) is distilled at the City of London Distillery, which is the first distillery to be commissioned in the City of London for over 200 years. Bottled at 40% ABV, it's another super citrus gin with orange, lemon and grapefruit in the mix. This translates nicely into an almost lavender-like softness with heaps of zesty, almost sharp notes. This is a great gin for a Collins – either the traditional Tom or any one of the newer-style fruit Collinses that are so easy to make.

CORK DRY GIN

Cork Dry Gin was first made at the Old Watercourse Distillery near Cork in 1793, using spices and herbs brought to the port of Cork, then a great centre of trade. It's now owned by Pernod Ricard and made at the Midleton Distilleries in County Cork. Although it's not rated by knowledgeable gin-drinkers because it is a cold compounded gin, there is something very mellow and Irish about its sherbety, soft citrus flavours. It is bottled at 38% ABV but far better at its export strength of 43% ABV. It is the biggest-selling gin in Ireland.

DARNLEY'S VIEW GIN

When the Wemyss family, renowned for their expertise in fine wines and spirits, were thinking of a name for their new gin they naturally thought of their historic family home Wemyss Castle in Scotland – the place where Mary Queen of Scots first spied her future husband, Lord Darnley, in 1565. Bottled at 40% ABV, Darnley's View contains elderflower, nicely balanced by a hefty dose of juniper. Darnley's View is the ideal summer gin and works very well in summery drinks like the Elderflower Collins and the Gin Fizz.

In 2012 Darnley's View Spiced Gin was launched. It contains cinnamon, nutmeg, cassia, Grains of Paradise, ginger, cumin and cloves. It's been joined by a Darnley's Navy Strength with the same botanicals and a bit more juniper at 57.1% ABV. At the same time all production has been moved up to Scotland to the very beautiful Kingsbarns Distillery where the Wemyss malt whisky is made. A charming Visitor Centre provides the opportunity to learn more about both gin and whisky production (*see* page 191 for details).

DEATH'S DOOR GIN

US-based Death's Door Spirits work with local farmers in Wisconsin to grow organic and sustainable grains and have become a leading force in craft distilling. Bottled at 47% ABV, Death's Door Gin is made from a mix of local organic hard red winter wheat and organic malted barley. Unusually, they distil the base spirit themselves at their small craft distillery and it is then re-distilled with three botanicals – juniper, coriander and fennel. Not surprisingly given this minimalist approach, juniper dominates, enhanced by the green notes of celery and coriander.

DODD'S GIN

Dodd's Gin is named after entrepreneur Ralph Dodd, who tried to raise capital to set up the London Distillery Company in the 1800s. He failed, but the London Distillery Company's new owners have gone from strength to strength. They recently moved across Battersea to the old Power Station where four stills produce more than 300,000 litres of gin a year.

Neutral spirit is infused with eight botanicals that include the unusual fresh lime peel, bay laurel, two types of cardamom, red raspberry leaf and honey from the nearby London Honey Company. On tasting there's spicy warmth from the cardamom with citrus and a pleasant viscosity, possibly from the use of the honey. The company also makes a bespoke gin for Fortnum & Mason.

FIFTY POUNDS

Crafted at Thames Distillers in London, Fifty Pounds Gin takes its name from the unsuccessful 1736 Gin Act when a £50 tax was levied on those wishing to produce and sell gin. Only two distilleries ever agreed to pay it!

It has 11 botanicals including eight of the classics, but the remaining three are a secret. The spirit is rested for three weeks after distillation to allow the flavour of the botanicals to marry. Bottled at 43.5% ABV, Fifty Pounds Gin's intense clean flavours have made it a hit with gin-loving barkeeps all over the world. On the nose there's massive juniper, lemon zest and sage aromas. On tasting there's a bit of sweetness and a juniper, orange and lemon citrus-led palate with fresh minty notes emerging in the finish.

FORDS GIN

Distilled in London at Thames Distillers, Fords Gin is a collaboration between eighth-generation Master Distiller Charles Maxwell and Simon Ford of the 86 Co.

It has a mix of nine botanicals including three different types of citrus, extra floral in the form of jasmine flower and extra spice in the form of cassia. The botanicals are steeped for 15 hours before distillation in 500-litre copper stills.

Fords Gin has been created with the classic gin drinks in mind. At a hefty 45% ABV it has the firepower to make its presence felt in all types of cocktails, whilst its elegant citrus notes make it a delightful everyday drinking gin.

FOXDENTON ESTATE 48 GIN

Foxdenton 48 is made at Thames Distillers in London for Nicholas Radclyffe, the sixth generation of his family to own the Foxdenton estate in Buckinghamshire. It's a classic London Dry that has been developed specifically for the G and T.

A simple recipe with six botanicals, its point of difference is the use of lime flower oil to add subtle citrus notes. Big juniper combined with a refreshing citrus kick delivers everything one would expect from a classic English gin. The Foxdenton Company also makes a range of excellent fruit gins – sloe, raspberry, plum, blackcurrant and damson.

GILBEY'S SPECIAL DRY GIN

Walter and Alfred Gilbey were the sons of a Bishops Stortford coach operator. Returning to London in 1857 from active duty in the Crimean War, the two brothers set up a wine business in Soho importing fine wines from the colonies to cater to the needs of the new, prosperous middle class. By 1867 they had done so well that they were able to move their premises to the famous Pantheon building in Oxford Street. At about the same time, realizing that gin was becoming middle-class too, they started producing gin at their Camden Town distillery (now a block of chic apartments).

Success was rapid and, by the 1920s, Gilbey's had gin distilleries in Australia and Canada. During Prohibition the Gilbey's empire flourished and the Pantheon offices regularly dispatched consignments of gin for shipment to Antwerp and Hamburg. From there they were shipped to just outside the 12-mile limit and then into the States for customers who paid cash.

So popular was Gilbey's gin during Prohibition that it was widely counterfeited. To prevent this, special frosted bottles were introduced; only in 1975 did the company revert to the original clear glass style. By this time Gilbey's had distilleries in New Zealand, Uruguay, Namibia, East Africa, Swaziland, Mauritius and Mozambique.

The Gilbey's brand is now owned by Diageo and is rarely seen on UK shelves. It is still produced under licence in the United States, however, by Jim Beam Brands, as well as in Australia, Canada, New Zealand and South Africa, and remains a huge brand in Commonwealth countries.

GIN MARE

Produced in a fishing village on Spain's Costa Dorado, Gin Mare bills itself as the gin of the Mediterranean. Here traditional botanicals are enhanced by the more unusual olives, basil, rosemary and thyme. Production is unconventional too, with all the botanicals save the citrus ones macerated individually in neutral grain alcohol, and then distilled in a copper pot still, again individually. Then all the botanicals are blended together and bottled at 42.7% ABV.

The result is very different from English-style gin: more like a juniper-flavoured schnapps with interesting herbal, savoury notes enhanced by the pungency of rosemary.

GORDON'S SPECIAL DRY GIN

Alexander Gordon was born in London on 10 August 1742. His father, George Gordon, was a native of Aberdeen, who allegedly left Scotland due to his involvement in the 1715 Jacobite uprising.

Alexander founded his distilling business in Southwark, in 1769, and then moved it, in 1786, to Clerkenwell. He had 10 children, one of whom, Charles, carried on the family business when Alexander died. His son, another Charles, sold the firm in 1878 to John Currie & Co.

Distillers at the Four Mills Distillery at Bromley by Bow, Currie & Co had provided Gordon's with spirit for rectification for many years. Tanqueray already had a close commercial relationship with Currie's and, in 1898, Gordon and Tanqueray combined to create Tanqueray, Gordon & Co. This move established the two companies as the most powerful force in English distilling, a position they still hold in the firm embrace of distilling giant Diageo.

Gordon's today is the global number-two-selling gin. Its UK base is Cameronbridge in Scotland but it also produces gin in the United States, Canada, South America and Jamaica.

Gordon's is a very traditional London Gin made to the original recipe which specifies ginger, cassia oil and nutmeg as well as the more commonly found juniper and coriander. Sold in the UK at 37.5% ABV, it is very juniper and lemon sherbety in a way that works well in a Gin and Tonic, which is how it's mostly drunk. Gordon's Export Strength at 47.3% ABV is a totally different experience – it's available in the UK as Gordon's Yellow Label and in worldwide duty-free and it's always worth seeking out. Gordon's has also launched new cucumber and elderflower-flavoured gins.

GREENALL'S ORIGINAL LONDON DRY

G & J Greenall has been producing gin since 1761, the year that Thomas Dakin built a distillery in the centre of Warrington, then a great centre for brewing and distilling. In 1870, Edward Greenall, a member of an established Lancashire brewing family, bought the Dakin company and acquired ownership of a successful business with an established distribution network.

In the mid-1960s, a new distillery, bottling facilities and warehouses were built on land close to the site of the original distillery. The company continued to expand and was chosen to create the Bombay family of gins. Disaster struck, in 2005, when the entire premises were almost destroyed by fire. The distillery was saved and continued to make a number of prestigious gins, in fact G&J Distillers are the UK's largest gin producers making many very good third-party own-label gins.

Their own brands are sometimes overlooked. Greenall's Original contains eight different botanicals, including the less common cassia bark and ground almonds. Bottled at 40% ABV, it's strongly citrus on the nose, developing into dry rounded juniper notes. The company also makes a range of Gin and Tonic in cans with huge markets in Eastern Europe, particularly in Russia, where people are seen downing them on the way to work. A recent addition to the Greenall's family is Thomas Dakin Gin based on an original Dakin recipe.

G'Vine gins are the brainchild of EuroWineGate, the French company who make Ciroc, the first vodka made from grapes, not grain or potatoes. They've extended the neutral wine spirit theory into gin production and G'Vine is made from Ugni Blanc grapes. The signature flavour of G'Vine Floraison is the rare vine flower, which blooms for a few days in June (this blossoming period is known in France as the floraison, hence the name). It is combined with other botanicals such as ginger root, liquorice, green cardamom, cassia bark, cubeb berries, nutmeg and lime. G'Vine Nouaison, named for the berry on the vine, has increased juniper and nutmeg, less vine flower and is bottled at a higher 43.9% ABV.

Whilst G'Vine gins may not be for the juniper purist, their light, floaty, floral flavours come to the fore in citrus-based drinks, especially when lime is in the mix.

HAYMAN'S GINS

The Haymans are one of the oldest English distilling families still involved in the trade and the current Chairman, Christopher, is the great-grandson of James Burrough who created Beefeater Gin in the 1800s. (The other even older gin family is that of Charles Maxwell, Master Distiller at Thames Distillers, whose gincestry goes back to the 1700s.) Rather like their illustrious ancestor, Hayman's Distillers make several different types of gin. Hayman's London Dry Gin is a fine example of the classic handcrafted London style. The mix of 10 botanicals is steeped with triple-distilled neutral grain spirit in a traditional pot still for 24 hours before distilling begins. The result is a crisp and elegant gin in which juniper, coriander and strong citrus elements are carefully balanced.

The company has also led the revival of Old Tom gin. Hayman's Old Tom is distilled from an original family recipe from the 1870s with more pungent botanicals like nutmeg, cassia bark, cinnamon and liquorice, and sweetened with sugar. It's an authentic re-creation of the Old Tom style once made by most English distillers, with one crucial difference: the spirit is properly rectified. It's much sought after by bartenders who want to experiment with original cocktail recipes from the glory days.

Hayman's 1820 Gin Liqueur is similar to the cordial gins of bygone days. It's made from 100% pure grain spirit and a subtle blend of botanicals with aromatic juniper and fruity notes. It should be drunk neat as a *digestif*.

Some years ago, when whisky experts William Grant & Sons decided to create a new gin, their inspiration was the traditional flavours of English summer. For months, the team worked in the lab, endlessly experimenting with different botanicals in the quest to get the right balance. After much trial and error, they arrived at the final botanicals – juniper, orris root, angelica, coriander, lemon and orange peel, caraway seeds, chamomile flowers, elderflowers, cubeb berries and meadowsweet with a final infusion of distilled oils of cucumber and Bulgarian *rosa damascena* (Damascus rose).

Having developed an unusual recipe, it's not surprising that William Grant should adopt a different approach to making their new baby. Hendrick's is small-batch distilled using two different methods – pot still and infusion. The two distillates are then combined and cucumber and rose distillates added.

The percentage of pot-distilled to infusion-distilled is part of its secret recipe. But the combination of strong, aromatic flavours achieved in a pot still with the more subtle, volatile flavours picked up in the Carterhead is obvious in the final taste of Hendrick's.

It results in fresh, floral, slightly aromatic notes, combined with silky smooth texture and mouthfeel. Hendrick's is one of the prime movers in gin's glorious renaissance as its lighter, more floral taste profile has opened up a raft of new drinking possibilities – not just the famous Hendrick's serve of a Gin and Tonic with a wedge of cucumber, but delicious summery drinks like the elderflower Martini as well.

JENSEN'S BERMONDSEY GIN

Jensen's Bermondsey Gin is the brainchild of Christian Jensen, a Danish IT specialist who fell in love with old-style gins while working in Japan and went on to develop his own gins – Jensen's Bermondsey Dry and Jensen's Old Tom. Production is now in a small distillery under a railway arch in Bermondsey, south London.

The original inspiration for the Jensen family of gins was from long forgotten London distilleries, with the emphasis on juniper-led flavours derived from ingredients used in the first London Dry gins of the 1800s. Bottled at 43% ABV, Jensen's Dry reportedly includes botanicals like sedge, liquorice, cinnamon, cardamom and bitter orange. It is a taste of the past with juniper the overriding flavour accompanied by citrus and soft spice.

Jensen's Old Tom gin, from an 1840s recipe, relies on natural flavouring, not sugar, for sweetness. Having tasted a 19th-century Old Tom Gin and seen recipes from that time detailing the amount of sugar used, it seems likely that some Old Tom gins used sugar and some did not. Whatever the source Jensen's Old Tom certainly has an attractive soft sweetness and its more aromatic style makes it a good choice for many of the classic gin drinks from the Golden Age of cocktails.

JUNIPER GREEN ORGANIC GIN

The world's first gin certified organic by the Soil Association, Juniper Green is distilled at the Thames Distillery in London. Juniper Green is a proper London Dry Gin. A simple recipe of organic juniper, coriander, angelica and savory is combined with an exceptionally clean spirit distilled from organic grain. And for those who are wheat-intolerant the extra good news is that it's 100% gluten-free.

On the palate Juniper Green is light and elegant, with a gentle burst of spice and strong juniper. Although it's annoying that the producers have chosen to follow Gordon's down the route of a 37.5% ABV, Juniper Green is constantly raved about in blind tastings and the lower alcoholic strength is reflected in competitive pricing. A stalwart everyday gin.

JUNIPERO GIN

Made by Anchor Distilling, who started the craft beer movement in the US, Junipero Gin is produced at a small distillery in San Francisco. It is a classic Dry style of gin made with 12 botanicals in a small copper pot still. Its makers are coy about the exact ingredients, but tasting reveals strong juniper, liquorice and grapefruit as well as other citrus. At 49.3% ABV, it's a big complex gin with a pronounced spiciness.

LARIOS GIN

Spain is a gin-lover's paradise, with the *Gin Tonica* the drink of choice – and what a choice, with literally hundreds of brands and different types of tonic water to experiment with. The only true locally made international brand is Larios, a gin that is very much in the London Dry style, ie double-distilled, aromatic and unsweetened with strong juniper flavours evident. Bottled at 40% ABV, it is drunk in vast quantities often in the famous Gin Larios con Coca-Cola, which is really rather good.

A premium expression, Larios 12, named after its 12 botanicals, contains nutmeg, angelica and masses of citrus in the form of lemon, orange, mandarin, tangerine, clementine, watermelon and lime. Here, the spirit and the botanicals are distilled together whilst a fifth distillation adds an infusion of orange blossom. Soft on the nose with hints of citrus developing into warm juniper and spice, try it with Coca-Cola but only the full-fat version, and make as you would a G and T.

MAGELLAN GIN

This French gin is named after the famous 16th-century Portuguese explorer Ferdinand Magellan. After his death in the Philippines, his ship reputedly returned laden with cloves. So the signature botanical of this rather stylish gin is cloves, accompanied by cinnamon, cassia, nutmeg and Grains of Paradise alongside the conventional gin botanicals. Made from triple-distilled French wheat that is re-distilled with the botanicals, the standout feature of this very elegant gin is its deep blue colour derived naturally from an infusion of iris. It's bottled at 44% ABV.

MARTIN MILLER'S GIN

The invention of the late Martin Miller, publisher of the famous *Miller's Antique Price Guides* and serial entrepreneur, Martin Miller's Gin is made at the Langley Distillery in a century-old gem of a copper pot still named "Angela". The botanicals recipe includes the less often used cassia and cinnamon bark, ground nutmeg and liquorice plus one other secret ingredient, almost certainly cucumber. Like all gins, Martin Miller's is reduced with demineralized water to its bottling strength of 40% ABV. This gin goes a bit further, taking the spirit on a 3,000-mile round trip to Iceland to be blended with what is considered to be the purest water on the planet. It may be this glacial water that makes Martin Miller's so exceptionally smooth and silky. What we end up with undoubtedly is a gentle gin with fragrant, slightly spicy aromas and strong hints of Parma violet and lavender. This unique taste profile makes Martin Miller's ideal in new-style cocktails like the Bramble.

MARTIN MILLER'S WESTBOURNE STRENGTH

Named after Martin Miller's original base in west London, Martin Miller's Westbourne Strength Gin is made identically to its sister brand but parts company in that it is bottled at the much higher 45.2% ABV. It's interesting to compare how much of a difference raising the alcoholic strength of a gin can make even when it's the same recipe. At 45.2% Westbourne Strength veers towards the more classic London flavour with lots of juniper, spice and citrus flavours.

MONKEY 47 GIN

Made by Black Forest Distillers in, yes, Germany's Black Forest (*Schwarzwald*), Monkey 47 is named for its alcoholic strength and the number of botanicals used in its recipe. The 47 include rarities such as spruce tips, cranberries, sage and verbena, many of which are handpicked in the Black Forest itself.

On tasting, the base spirit appears more aromatic and less "neutral" than the grain spirit used in British gins, but that could also be explained by the diversity of the botanical flavourings. Aromatic and herbal, Monkey 47 is reminiscent of old-style gins that had a stronger connection to Dutch genever. Which makes it the perfect gin to experiment with in original Golden Age cocktails – especially ones with vermouth and/or bitters.

NO. 3 ST. JAMES'S LONDON DRY GIN

When the renowned wine and spirits merchants Berry Bros & Rudd create a gin, one can be confident it will be top-quality. No. 3 Gin is named for the company's famous shop in St James Street in the heart of London, founded in 1698 by the Widow Bourne. That original shop is still the oldest wine and spirit merchant in the UK and a Mecca for lovers of fine drink. It still has the original scales that were also used to weigh the shop's many notable customers, such as Lord Byron, Horatio Nelson, Lady Hamilton and William Pitt.

Made in Schiedam, Holland's distilling centre and gin's ancestral home, No. 3 is the Platonic ideal of a classic London Dry Gin bottled at a serious 46% ABV. The botanical mix of juniper, coriander, sweet orange peel, angelica, grapefruit peel and cardamom is left to steep overnight before distillation in traditional copper pot stills. On the nose there's a welcome blast of piney juniper with citrus and coriander very evident. In the mouth the juniper develops into a crispness nicely balanced by gentle cardamom spiciness. Perfect for a Dry Martini and a Negroni where one wants big, bold flavours.

NO. 209 GIN

No. 209 Gin is made in San Francisco in a specially commissioned Scottish copper pot still based on the design of the Glenmorangie whisky stills, which were in fact originally used for making gin. It's a robust gin, built around the signature botanicals of bergamot, sweet orange, cardamom and cassia as well as the more usual juniper and citrus. On the palate are pleasant lavender and floral notes that combine well with the bittersweet juniper. It's a favourite of bartenders who recommend No. 209 in a Gin Mojito.

OPIHR GIN

A spiced gin, Opihr Oriental Gin references the fabled port of Biblical times and the centuries-old spice route from the Far East. Made in the more prosaic surrounding of Warrington by Quintessential, it has been developed by Master Distiller Joanne Moore, one of the UK's two female head distillers. Lots of spice – cubebs from Indonesia, cumin from Turkey, and cardamom, ginger and black pepper from India, combine to produce aromatic and warming flavours. Spice and juniper are perfectly balanced and coriander also comes through strongly. Works well when mixed with the extra spice of ginger beer and also in a punch.

Bacardi-owned Oxley Spirits Company spent eight years developing Oxley Gin and, along the way, introduced a whole new way of distilling gin. In a major technological advance, it is the first-ever spirit created by cold distillation. So instead of heat being applied to reduce the spirit and botanicals to vapour, vacuum is used to reduce the pressure in the still and lower the temperature to approximately –5° C. At this temperature the spirit, which has been macerated for 15 hours, becomes vapour. It then meets a cold finger probe (chilled to –100° C) and reverts back to liquid to be collected for bottling.

All this is done under the careful eye of Charles Maxwell of Thames Distillers. The bespoke still at London's Thames Distillers produces only 120 bottles per batch and the actual distillation takes only around two hours. One of the major advantages of cold distillation is that there is no need to make a cut in the run.

There are no feints or foreshots to be discarded because the rate of flavour extraction from the botanicals is the same at the beginning of the run as it is at the end. As a result there is almost no wastage compared with traditional distillation methods.

But all this technical wizardry would be meaningless without some real impact on flavour. And here Oxley delivers big time. The 14 botanicals include the traditional ones as well as three different types of fresh citrus – grapefruit, orange and lemon – and exotics like vanilla and meadowsweet. Slightly spicy on the nose with hints of lavender, almond, marshmallow and soft citrus, juniper is evident but not dominant. Think soft and scented rather than oily and pungent.

What stand out, however, are the exceptionally clean and fresh flavours and the texture and purity of the spirit that is holding these complex aromas in harmony. At 47% ABV Oxley is an intense, flavourful gin and it's one of the few gins that can happily be drunk neat over ice in a balloon glass ideally with a grapefruit twist.

Plymouth Gin has a long but sometimes unreliable history. Legend has it that the Distillery Building in Southside Street was the former monastery of an order of Dominicans, hence the name Black Friars, but that is largely discounted, as there is no record of a Dominican monastery in Plymouth. We do know that Black Friars became in turn the town's Marshalsea or debtors' prison, the first Non-Conformist meeting place and a billet for Huguenot refugees. The Pilgrim Fathers are reputed to have spent their last night in England here before they set sail on the *Mayflower*.

A deed of sale dated 12 November 1697 refers to a "mault-house" at Black Friars and it's pretty clear that Black Friars was used for making alcohol from the birth of legal commercial distilling in England. When distilling was deregulated in 1690, malting grain, brewing, distilling and rectifying (the process of re-distilling spirit to make gin) were complementary activities, often carried out under the same roof. Only in 1825 did it become illegal to produce the base spirit and re-distilled gin at the same location.

The *Pigot's Trade Directory* of 1822 lists Fox, Coates and Williams as distillers at Southside Street too. It's possible they were there earlier and it is likely that there was still a brewery, Brittan Brewers, on the site as evidenced by a title deed of 1825. An 1842 legal document records the lease of a property in Southside Street by Mark Stephens Grigg and W. H. Hawker who were partners in the distillers now known as Coates & Co.

William Henry Hawker had joined the business in 1832. His grandson, Francis Ford Freeman, followed him into the company and, until the 1950s Coates & Co was a private company, owned and managed by the closely connected descendants of the Hawker and Freeman families, later joined by other cousins, the Mays.

Plymouth Gin then became part of an undignified and complicated pass the parcel game amongst bigger drinks companies until it was rescued in 1996 by a group of private investors headed up by serial entrepreneur Charles Rolls of Fever-Tree mixer fame. Plymouth Gin is now owned by Pernod Ricard.

There is a great misconception that Plymouth is a different "style" of gin. It isn't, it's made in exactly the same way as a London Dry but it does not carry the London Dry label. In fact it used to be the only UK gin to have a protected geographic designation, a bit like an EU *appellation controllée*. This does not relate to its production methods but is the result of a series of legal verdicts in the 1880s when Coates & Co won several suits under the "passing off" legislation, establishing that Plymouth Gin could only be made within Plymouth city walls, by law. The company has decided not to renew its protected status under EU law for the very good reason that it is technically impossible for any other gin to be made in Plymouth and be able to describe itself as "Plymouth Gin".

Produced in a still that has stood for over 150 years, Plymouth Gin has a subtle, full-bodied flavour with no bitter botanicals. A higher than usual proportion of root ingredients is the source of Plymouth's distinctive, earthy, rooty tastes, whilst the addition of sweet orange and cardamom imparts a softly fruity, spicy finish. Pure water from Dartmoor contributes to its exceptionally clean and fresh flavour. Plymouth Original is bottled at 41.2% ABV whilst Plymouth Navy Strength at a whopping 57% ABV. Plymouth also produces Sloe Gin and Damson Gin and an exceptionally smooth Fruit Cup.

The gin of the Royal Navy, the gin of the world's first Martini recipe, Sir Winston Churchill's favourite gin and once the biggest-selling English gin brand in the world, Plymouth Gin is a true hero of the gin movement. It also boasts the UK's first ever Gin Distillery Visitor Centre where you can learn all you ever need to know about gin – (*see Gin Places* on page 191).

PORTOBELLO ROAD NO. 171 GIN

Above the Portobello Star bar along London's famous Portobello Road is the Ginstitute, the smallest gin museum in London, the home of gin. Most importantly it also contains the city's smallest working copper pot still – "Coppernicus". Owners Ged Feltham and Jake Burger devised their gin recipe here and it is now commercially produced at nearby Thames Distillers in Clapham.

Portobello Road No. 171 uses nine botanicals, majoring on warm spice botanicals like cassia bark, liquorice and nutmeg. Citrus in the form of lemon and bitter orange comes through strongly and somehow, although there is neither cardamom nor grapefruit in the recipe, one picks up hints of aromatic cardamom and grapefruit on the nose. At 42% ABV, Portobello comes into its own in tonic water where robustness is required. *See Gin Places* on page 190 for further information on the Ginstitute.

BELOW: *This sign is inside the bar at No. 171 Portobello Road in west London. As well as the bar, there is a working distillery and a museum (the Ginstitute) on the premises.*

SACRED GIN

The Sacred Distillery in London's Highgate is actually located in founder Ian Hart's back garden, so it could not be more micro. The gin is made with 12 botanicals including lemon and lime, cardamom, nutmeg, and a very unusual botanical, Boswellia Sacra (aka frankincense) from which the product derives its name.

The distillation process is unusual too as, instead of a traditional copper pot still, Sacred is made under low-pressure vacuum. Each of the 12 botanicals is distilled separately using English grain spirit and then blended to make the final spirit, which is bottled at 40% ABV. The idea here is that separate, low-pressure, low-temperature distillations are able to extract maximum flavour from each different botanical.

On tasting Sacred is lush and fruity with very big and clean flavours and slightly scented notes derived from the frankincense. It works well with cranberry juice and bitter lemon. The company also produce a Gin Blending Kit that allows gin-lovers to blend their own gin as well as a very delicious gin-based Rosehip Cup.

SEAGRAM'S GINS

Seagram's Extra Dry is the US equivalent of Gordon's in the UK – a huge-volume brand that outsells its nearest competitors by a country mile. For that reason, it is not appreciated as much as it really ought to be. Known as "the smooth gin in the bumpy bottle", it's made in the USA from 100% American grain neutral spirit that is distilled with juniper, coriander, orris, angelica, cardamom and cassia bark. It is then mellowed in charred white oak barrels, which gives it a slightly golden hue. It has candied fruit, citrus and juniper on the nose, then a slightly sweet sherbet palate with spice and floral hints and is bottled at 40% ABV.

Seagram's Distiller's Reserve is the combination of the best of the barrels as selected by the Master Distiller. The higher strength of the spirit at 51% ABV is definitely noticeable when it is sipped straight.

SIPSMITH LONDON DRY GIN

Sipsmith London Dry Gin is produced in Chiswick in three bespoke copper pot stills – Prudence, Patience and Constance. The spirit is made by hand in genuinely small batches, never more than 500 bottles a time, often considerably less, by Master Distiller and well-known cocktail historian Jared Brown. Those kinds of volumes may have to change as the company has been acquired by drinks giant Beam Suntory.

I take a fond interest in Sipsmith's fortunes as I first introduced Brown to Sipsmith founders Sam Galsworthy and Fairfax Hall at the Beefeater Distillery. They were the first people I knew who said "we want to make our own gin". I knew they would succeed.

The family includes the signature 41.6% ABV Sipsmith London Dry. There's no swinging from the chandeliers here in terms of flavour – it is a classic London Dry Gin. Its botanicals include the familiar ones as well as liquorice, ground almonds, cassia bark and cinnamon. The aromas are of citrus with a meadow-like herbaceousness. On the palate it opens up to distinctive juniper, sweet orange and lemon marmalade, making it ideal for a Gin and Tonic or Gin Collins. They produce sloe and damson gins as well as a Summer Cup, a new take on a Pimm's-style fruit cup and Lemon Drizzle gin.

What got everyone talking is the Sipsmith VJOP (very junipery over proof) gin, a wow at 57.5% ABV. Extra juniper is added by suspending perforated balls filled with juniper above the spirit and capturing their flavours through vapour infusion. Extra juniper is also added to the mix before distilling.

Bramley and Gage, the producers of 6 O'Clock Gin, are a perfect example of how small, rural-based family businesses are often at the forefront of the great gin revival, not necessarily the hipsters. Starting out on a fruit farm in south Devon the family started diversifying in the mid-1980s by making a range of strawberry, raspberry and blackcurrant liqueurs. The fruit came from their own farm and the recipes followed a "maceration" method similar to that practised in France. The liqueurs met with great success and were soon available in local off licences, delicatessens and tourist attractions. Shortly afterwards Bramley's Sloe Gin was launched to great acclaim.

Fast forward to 2010 with the family business now under the management of a younger generation and the release of 6 O'Clock Gin. It's a refinement of the gin that is the basis for the company's fruit gins, and it's made in a bespoke still in a small distillery near Bristol. It is literally a breath of fresh air with a simple recipe of seven botanicals including elderflower and savoury and bottled at a respectable 43% ABV. Exceptionally clean and fresh in the mouth it combines the traditional juniper character of gin with graceful floral notes.

Bramley and Gage were also well ahead of the curve when it comes to boutique tonic water. Unable to find a tonic water to suit their gin they launched their own some years ago. 6 O'Clock Tonic is all natural with no saccharine or sodium benzoate. Instead natural quinine extracts with infusions of lemon and lime create a clean-tasting not over-sweet mixer. The company continues to produce a range of fruit liqueurs and vermouths.

TANQUERAY

Charles Tanqueray, born in 1810, was the descendant of Huguenots and came from a long line of clergymen. The distilling business of Edward & Charles Tanqueray & Co, Rectifiers, was established by 1838 on Vine Street at the southern edge of Bloomsbury. However, according to a property deed of the same year, the site had been used as a distillery for some time.

In his Bloomsbury Distillery, Charles Tanqueray wanted to produce a quality gin, and after years of experimentation, he finally produced his unique recipe. Tanqueray Gin met with instant success and a prestigious clientele. Soon, Tanqueray stoneware crocks, used in the trade until 1900, were seen in the better class of grocer and wine and spirit merchants as well as in discerning households. (He did not deal in bulk-casked gin for ordinary taverns.) Within a few years, Tanqueray Gin was being exported to the British colonies while still much in demand at home.

Tanqueray and Gordon's joined forces in 1898. In the 1950s the decision was taken to focus Tanqueray on the export market, particularly the US where it was the favourite tipple of celebrities such as Bob Hope, Frank Sinatra and Sammy Davis Junior. Frustratingly this meant that for many years Tanqueray was barely available in the UK, but one of the benefits of the great gin revival has been the relaunch of Tanqueray on its home turf.

Today, the Tanqueray name is found on three quite different gins ...

TANQUERAY RANGPUR

Tanqueray Rangpur stirred up controversy in the bartender community and it has not gone away. Is it a fruit gin? Why is it so sweet? Where's the juniper? I've never seen the problem: if you like citrus-heavy gins, and I do, this is the most citrusy, limey gin you'll encounter.

Made with fresh Rangpur limes – a hybrid of a lemon and a mandarin and not a lime at all – there's also juniper, coriander, ginger, kaffir limes and bay leaves. The limes are described as being "sequentially distilled", i.e. added to the still later in the run. For me Rangpur falls between a traditional Dry and a fruit gin with a distinctive lime taste. Mix with cranberry juice for a Rangpur Cran or with ginger ale and a few drops of bitters for a Rangpur Ginger.

All Tanqueray UK gins are made at Diageo's distilleries in Scotland, at Cameronbridge. The Tanqueray family now includes a fine limited edition Old Tom Gin made by adding unaged grain spirit and beet sugar to its London Dry recipe. A Tanqueray Bloomsbury Edition based on one of Charles Tanqueray's original recipes launched in 2015, a farewell gift from retiring Master Distiller Tom Nichol.

TANQUERAY SPECIAL DRY GIN

Tanqueray Special Dry Gin is a London Dry with knobs on, greeting one boisterously with a lovely juniper-fresh welcome. Although the recipe is still secret, Special Dry is believed to contain only four botanicals – juniper, coriander, angelica and liquorice – proof that sometimes more is less and that the balance of ingredients is key to taste. On tasting, juniper and liquorice are very obvious as is a subtle spiciness most likely derived from coriander.

In contrast with the Export strength of 47.3% ABV, the Special Dry is bottled at 43.1% ABV which somehow suits the character of the recipe better.

TANQUERAY No. TEN

A radical addition to the gin category when it launched in 2000, Tanqueray No. Ten was created specifically for Martinis. Made in small batches in a swan neck still known as "Tiny Ten", it adds fresh citrus in the form of limes, oranges and grapefruit as well as chamomile to the botanical mix. The more volatile citrus is distilled first with pure grain spirit and then re-distilled with the traditional Tanqueray botanicals. Extra fresh citrus is added to the final spirit. Juniper is at the heart of this gin, but is relatively laid-back when compared to big gins like Tanqueray Special Dry. It's very citrusy, clean and as fresh as a meadow with soothing notes of chamomile.

THE BOTANIST

Another supreme example of Scottish distilling know-how from the Bruichladdich distillery on Islay, The Botanist is described as an "Islay Dry Gin". It is very much a product of the Hebrides as 21 out of the 31 botanicals used grow locally. The list of native botanicals is almost bewildering and includes apple mint, birch leaves, bog myrtle leaves, chamomile, thistle flowers, elderflowers, gorse flowers, heather, hawthorn flowers and mugwort leaves. These are added to more traditional gin botanicals and distilled in a low-pressure Lomond pot still. At 46% ABV The Botanist is an intense and very complex gin but retains a strong juniper character despite the number of botanical flavourings used. Clean, bone-dry with subtle floral and herbal flavours, it lends itself to Martinis and many of the new-style fruit-based Collinses.

THE LONDON No 1

The London No 1 Gin is unusual in that it's blue, the colour being derived from an infusion of gardenia flowers. Its base is a spirit made from Suffolk and Norfolk grain re-distilled with 13 botanicals including liquorice root, savory, cinnamon and cassia bark. London No 1 Gin also features bergamot, that instantly recognizable perfumed aroma so familiar in Earl Grey tea. Rested for three weeks after distillation in a pot still, the result is a very English-style Distilled Gin. At a generous 47% ABV, The London Gin is elegant on the nose with marked spicy and balsamic notes. Soft, elegant and mellow in the mouth with a lingering spiciness, it's a sophisticated, well-rounded gin with slightly perfumed qualities that make it an ideal partner for cranberry juice.

Warner Edwards Harrington Gin is made in a barn on a farm in Northamptonshire using locally grown botanicals such as elderflower and lavender. Most of the water used for reduction is from a local spring. So it couldn't be more local and more in tune with the trend for proving provenance. At 44% ABV it has a spicy fragrant core with lots of mellow sweetness.

WHITLEY NEILL LONDON DRY

Whitley Neill is a premium London Dry Gin, created by Johnny Neill, the fourth generation of the Greenall Whitley distilling family. It's made from a 100% grain spirit that is steeped with the botanicals prior to distillation in antique copper pot stills. The recipe took some time to formulate as the producers were determined to bring something new to the party. The result is nine botanicals consisting of core botanicals and the addition of two signature elements from Africa – the Cape gooseberry and the fruit of the Baobab tree, the tree of life. The taste experience starts with a spicy freshness on the nose. Laid-back juniper and citrus combine with the fresh tanginess of the wild fruit to create robust yet delicate and clean flavours. A pleasant lingering finish holds those flavours in the mouth whilst an alcoholic strength of 42% ABV ensures perfect balance.

XORIGUER GIN DE MAHON

A bit of an oddity, Xoriguer Gin de Mahon is one of only two gins with a protected geographic status (the other is Vilnius Gin from Lithuania). It can only be made in Mahon on the Balearic island of Menorca. Gin distilling there dates from the British presence in the 18th century when Menorca was an important British naval base. British soldiers and sailors stationed in Mahon wanted gin, the fashionable spirit at home, so enterprising local distilleries started making it from juniper berries distilled with a spirit made from the local wine.

The Xoriguer distillery, founded and still owned by the Pons family, is now the only gin distillery on the island. There, Gin de Mahon is made, as it always has been, from a wine distillate in ancient copper stills heated by wood-burning fires. Once distilled, it is stored in large oak barrels and bottled at 40% ABV.

Only members of the Pons family know the exact ingredients of the Xoriguer recipe. It certainly has juniper and other aromatic herbs. Tasting reveals a brandy-like flavour with notes of caraway, fennel and orris. Xoriguer Gin is sold in green glass bottles with handles that copy old Dutch stone genever crocks. It is drunk widely on the island, particularly during the summer-long season of fiestas when it is mixed with lemonade in a drink called Pomada. It tastes innocuous but be warned, it packs a real punch – as the many British visitors to Menorca can attest.

ZUIDAM GIN

Given the ever-increasing popularity of London-style gin it's no wonder that Dutch distillers are reclaiming the distilling high ground and turning their attention to gin. There are quite a few brands of Dutch London Dry-style gin on the market but this high-strength 44.5% ABV Dry Gin from the family-owned Zuidam Distillers in Holland stands out. It contains nine botanicals – fresh sweet oranges and lemons, not the more conventional peels, whole bean vanilla, liquorice root and cardamom. The result is a big gin, strong in juniper but with a fiery sweetness.

SMALL BATCH GIN

———◆◆◆◆———

Because gin is relatively straightforward to produce and does not require ageing, new gin-lovers are making the stuff not just drinking it. From Orkney to Cornwall, and all over Europe, hundreds of small distilleries have sprung up. Some are waiting for other spirits to mature, others are purely driven by a passion for making the best gin possible. It's an exciting time of experimentation and innovation.

This section is not called Craft Gins. I think the word "craft" is a lazy catch-all for a more interesting phenomenon that could be summed up as experimental, small batch, independent distillers doing it for themselves. All gin is crafted. Try telling gin Titans like Desmond Payne of Beefeater, Sean Harrison of Plymouth and Tom Nichol of Tanqueray, that all this time they have really been making what? industrial gin. I don't think so.

Given that probably hundreds of gin brands have been launched in the past two years alone, it would be futile to try and review and update all of them. That's what the Internet is for and there are many excellent, if slightly geeky, websites doing that. This Directory, instead, is a carefully curated selection of gins I believe are the most interesting, either because they have an intriguing back story, or they are made in an unusual way or simply, in my opinion, they taste superb. Inevitably there will be some glaring omissions, given the fast-moving pace of the category, but think of it as a snapshot of gin now.

The Arbikie Distillery, perched on the east coast of Angus, is the brainchild of the three Stirling brothers whose family have farmed here since the 1660s. With their unique field-to-glass ethos they are reviving the earliest traditions of commercial distilling when, all over Europe, distilling was a cottage industry, the ideal way to make the most of surplus crops and earn income during bleak winters.

In addition to whisky and vodka the Arbikie distillery makes two gins: AK's Gin and Kirsty's Gin. A major investment has seen the installation of both pot and column stills to enable all the base spirit used to be produced on site. At Arbikie they plant the seeds that grow into the crops that are harvested from the fields outside the distillery and are then distilled. Such is the commitment to traceability here, that each bottle carries the name of the crop strain used and the name of the field in which it grows!

Kirsty's Gin combines familiar botanicals with kelp, carline thistle root and blaeberries, three ingredients drawn from the stunningly beautiful landscape of this part of Scotland. It's based on a neutral alcohol derived from potatoes and is bottled at 43% ABV. On the nose there is a sharp fruitiness and big pine hit. The flavours develop further with hints of eucalyptus and a pleasant earthiness perhaps also derived from the potato-based spirit.

AK's Gin is composed of 10 botanicals including the less common thistle, black pepper, black cardamom, calamus root, mace and local honey. Wheat spirit is the backbone of this gin, underpinning its spicy character with a slightly sweet nuttiness.

BRIGHTON GIN

Produced in Brighton's first ever legal distillery, Brighton Gin is an ode to the city itself, celebrating everything about this bohemian enclave from its freewheeling spirit to the particular aqua shade of the railings on Brighton Pier, also the colour of the distinctive bottle livery. Although it's technically a London Dry, Brighton Gin prefers to focus on its unique location and indeed, it is as English as a day at the seaside complete with a Kiss Me Quick hat.

Inside is even more important than what is outside. I have to declare an interest here as Brighton Gin is exactly the kind of gin I really like – strongly citrus, clearly juniper with lots of soft green notes and totally refreshing. I am not alone in my tastes as Brighton Gin took the top spot as The People's Choice Gin in the 2017 People's Drinks Awards.

It is made from 100% British organic wheat spirit that is re-distilled with juniper, fresh orange and lime peel, locally grown coriander seed (the first UK commercially grown coriander seed in over 200 years) and milk thistle, foraged wild on the South Downs and famous for helping to restore liver function. So no hangovers then, unless of course…

Bottled at a reliable 40% ABV, Brighton Gin has won several quality awards since its launch in 2014 from a tiny location in the back of a pub. Owing to demand the team have now expanded to a much larger distillery but have retained a charming artisan ethos. Try it with a slice of fresh orange in a G and T or in a Rocktail, a G and T garnished with a piece of actual Brighton rock.

BURLEIGH'S LONDON DRY GIN

Master Distiller Jamie Baxter is a prime mover in the great gin renaissance, having built 17 distilleries or around 5% of all the new distilleries that have opened in the UK in the past 10 years. An impressive, indeed unique record: so, when he decided to build his own distillery and launch his own gin, expectations were high. They have not been disappointed.

Bawdon Lodge Farm, deep in the wilds of Leicestershire's Charnwood Forest, is the home of the 45 West Distillery and Burleighs London Dry Gin. Here in a converted milking shed the recipe for the first in what turned out to be a range of classically crafted gins was created. Inspiration came from a walk in nearby Burleigh Wood when Baxter came across clumps of silver birch, dandelion, burdock, elderberry and iris growing wild. These arboreal flavours are at the heart of Burleigh's London Dry Gin. Bottled at a very straightforward 40% ABV, it has a dry juniper freshness followed by pine, citrus zest and eucalyptus. There are also intriguing earthy, spicy and floral notes in the background. In short a big, bold gin that delivers in all respects.

At the same time Baxter had developed another recipe that he personally loved but was perhaps a little less accessible. It morphed into Burleigh's Distillers Cut, a more Old Tom style of gin with natural sweetness derived from botanicals such as liquorice and orris root. The full range now includes an Export Strength at 47% ABV, the Pink Edition made with preserved cherry blossom from Japan and the Leicester City edition, a joint venture with Leicester City Football Club.

The Burleigh's family of gins is an excellent example of what happens when distilling expertise, creativity and passion combine. And, if you want to see the master at work the Distillery also runs a very successful Gin School and a programme of Tours and Tastings – *see Gin Places* on page 190 for contact details.

Burleigh's
LONDON DRY
GIN
MADE IN ENGLAND
70cl℮ 40%vol

Made in the UK at Thames Distillers for Sri Lankan-based Rockland Distilleries, Colombo 7 Gin has a fascinating back story.

Rockland was established in 1924 in order to produce good-quality arrack, the national drink of Ceylon, as the country was then. When the Second World War broke out all trade routes were disrupted and British-made gin no longer found its way to the thirsty expats of the island. Rockland founder Carl de Silva Wijeyeratne decided to make a local gin with specific Sri Lankan spices and came up with the botanical recipe for what is now Colombo 7 using distinctive local spices such as Sri Lankan cinnamon bark, Sri Lankan curry leaves and ginger root.

At this time however it was not permitted to make gin or indeed any other "non native" spirit outside the UK. Persistent lobbying from Rockland Distilleries resulted in the formation of a new regulation called Ceylon Made Foreign Liquor (CMFL), which allowed the production of gin and other "non native" spirits in Sri Lanka (then Ceylon) and the manufacture of Colombo Gin. Incidentally this ruling was also implemented in India, creating Indian Made Foreign Liquor around the same time.

When the war ended and normal trade resumed the company began to make a more traditional London Dry-style gin, Rockland Dry, still the biggest-selling gin in the country. The original recipe for Colombo 7 was rediscovered by a new generation of the Wijeyeratne family and, in 2015, the decision was made to relaunch the recipe and, because of political uncertainty, have it produced in the UK. Most importantly it's now made from a grain spirit, which is obviously hard to source in Sri Lanka then and now.

With a 43.1% ABV strength, Colombo 7, despite its exotic ingredients, is very firmly in the London Dry style. Lots of exuberant pepper and spice with lovely warming notes are the keynote flavours, and whilst cinnamon can often overpower a botanical recipe, here it is present in a gentlemanly fashion. Ideal in a classic G and T garnished with curry leaves.

COLONSAY GIN

In August 2016 Finlay and Eileen Geekie, moved to the tiny island of Colonsay off Scotland's wild west Coast, to start a new life and establish Wild Thyme Spirits. The distillery on the island is now up and running and producing its first batch of Colonsay Gin. There's also an exciting partnership with the Colonsay Estate to hand-forage for botanicals on the island, including access to the highly acclaimed gardens and grounds of Colonsay House. This gives the distillers scope to experiment with a huge array of local botanicals to help create products with unmistakable Colonsay provenance.

The flagship Colonsay Gin botanical recipe consists of juniper, angelica root, orris root, coriander, liquorice, orange peel and the slightly unusual calamus root, more commonly found in herbal medicine. Distilled in a traditional pot still, the also unusual bottling strength of 47% ABV is the result of experimentation with different alcoholic strengths and it was identified as being best for carrying the full flavour of this particular botanical recipe.

On nosing and tasting, the juniper forward character of Colonsay is apparent. It's complemented by hints of lavender and green notes of coriander with a pleasant ginger-like warmness from the calamus. This superbly-crafted gin shines in a G and T – the distillers recommend a garnish of a sliver of green chilli, and it works.

The Geekies share their passion for gin through a programme of Gin Lover's Retreats hosted at their small hotel on Colonsay. With more than 200 gins to explore and a wild island to discover it's the perfect opportunity to broaden your gin horizons.

COTSWOLDS DRY GIN

The Cotswolds Distillery is the creation of Daniel Szor, a former City hedge fund manager who dreamed of making whisky in the heart of the English countryside. In 2012 he employed some of the most experienced whisky distillers in Scotland to advise on the building of the distillery. It's now up and running with the first release of matured whisky from local Cotswolds barley made available in 2017.

Gin was an obvious step for the Cotswold Distillery and the starting point was the use of lavender from nearby Snowshill. To this signature flavour is added bay leaf, grapefruit, lime, black pepper and cardamom and the more conventional gin botanicals. This mix enters the still at roughly 10 times the weight of a normal botanical to spirit ratio and the still is only filled to the three-quarters mark to ensure vapours get more contact with the copper during distillation.

Cotswold Dry is cut fairly early in the run and the liquid is rested for five days to allow the various flavours to bed down. Then water is added to reduce the strength to 46% ABV. Because Cotswold Dry is not chill-filtered it retains a rich and robust mouthfeel and a pearlescent "louche" or cloudiness appears when you add ice or tonic. Although purists might cavil, it's all part of this gin's singular charm.

On tasting the first impression is of lavender enhancing the camphor lavender notes in juniper then a herbaceous rush. Bright citrus notes also come to the fore. There's a hefty dose of spice and clean, long finish.

The Cotswold range also includes a barrel-aged limited-edition bottling, 1616, to commemorate the 400th anniversary of Shakespeare's death, made with a 55% malt 45% grain spirit so similar to genever. Cotswold Hedgerow Gin is a fruit gin made with sloes, damsons, bullace and blackberries all foraged locally and is drunk as one would sloe gin, either neat, or in cocktails.

DAFFY'S GIN

Daffy's Gin launched at the beginning of 2015 and has very quickly made its mark, winning numerous awards and widespread distribution. The Strathmashie Estate in the Cairngorms National Park is now home to the distillery, carefully, not to say obsessively, overseen by its owner, Irishman Chris Molyneux.

There's a quite astonishing level of detail applied to the whole process of making Daffy's. It is accepted practice that most small distilleries buy in neutral grain spirit from specialist producers to ensure consistent quality. Not Daffy's, who specify a wheat spirit made in Normandy under the direct supervision of the Daffy's team, who even select which crops are to be used. Back home in the Highlands this spirit is placed in an ancient alembic 500-litre still along with the botanicals and left to macerate for a full four days before distillation. Again unusual, but the distillers believe this is the best way to ensure full hydration of the botanicals.

In many ways Daffy's is a classic London Dry gin with familiar gin flavourings but there's a twist comes with the addition of Lebanese mint as a signature botanical. It's a particular form of mint that grows only in the Bekaa Valley of Lebanon and there's no question that it brings loads to this flavour party.

On tasting there's a quite startling brightness and freshness with juniper, citrus and fresh mint the dominant flavours. In the background is that sharp Dentyne flavour of cassia blending beautifully with other spice notes. Recommended G and T serve is with fresh mint and lime: lots of lime actually, at least three thick wedges.

The company has also set up the Strathmashie Gin School and Visitor Centre (*see Gin Places* on page 191 for details).

The East London Liquor Company is housed in a former glue factory in Mile End. The location is significant as during the last Gin Craze, East London was home to dozens of distilleries, including the famous Three Mills Distillery at nearby Bromley by Bow, home to what is still the largest tidal mill in the world. But the gin made now at east London's Grove Road is quite different to the rotgut that fuelled the squalor of 18th-century London.

Entry to the Distillery is via a bar behind which specially commissioned copper Holstein stills gently do their job combining both the more traditional "boiling" method of distillation with vapour infusion. There are three gins in the portfolio, all made with a 100% British wheat spirit from the Langley Distillery. Everything else, including the bottling, is done on site.

The botanicals in their signature London Dry include lemon and grapefruit peel, cubeb berries and cardamom. Then there's Premium Batch No. 1 bottled at a higher strength of 47% ABV with no citrus ingredients but extra spice in the form of cassia bark. Premium Batch No. 2 is completely different again – very herbaceous with classic English garden ingredients such as lavender, fennel seeds, thyme, winter savoury and sage. All gin-drinking options are covered from the G and T to the Martini to a deliciously herbal Negroni with many others in between.

Being small allows the guys to be experimental, even playful. They launched a range of barrel-ageing gins that sees the different core gin expressions aged in different types of wooden cask to produce limited editions of aged gin. In addition to gin they also produce small batch whisky, rum and vodka.

Eden Mill is a rare beast in that it is one of the very few UK distilleries that make gin, whisky and beer in the same location, a former paper mill, just outside St. Andrews in Fife. The place has a long association with distilling as, in the 19th century, it was home to the Haig family's whisky distillery.

When it comes to gin Eden Mill are not afraid to experiment and the gin portfolio currently includes four very different expressions – Eden Mill Original, Eden Mill Oak, Eden Mill Love and Eden Mill Hop.

The Original at 42% ABV makes use of seabuckthorn berries that grow within walking distance of the distillery. This tart berry flavour is smoothed out with green juniper and other citrus from lemon balm and lemon peel. Eden Mill Oak incorporates hickory chips from used golf clubs and goes big on spice whilst Eden Mill Love turns pink when tonic water is added and is bursting with floral, dare I say girly, flavours. Eden Mill Hop, at a hefty 46% ABV, is made with Australian Galaxy Hops. The company also produces an interesting range of gin liqueurs and RTD cocktails and has a very well regarded Visitor Centre. So, something for everyone.

The distillery facilities at Eden Mill are on course to double in size over the next few years and there's no doubt there's a whole load more action and experimentation to come from these Scottish pioneers.

EDINBURGH GIN

Edinburgh Gin is a juniper-led gin with a strong Scottish provenance although initially it wasn't made in Scotland. Having been acquired by Ian Macleod Distillers it is now appropriately made in its own bespoke distillery in Edinburgh.

At the Biscuit Factory in Leith, Scottish grain spirit is distilled together with classic gin botanicals and the addition of distinctively Scottish flavours such as locally grown juniper, milk thistle and heather. Finally it is bottled at 43% ABV. On the nose, the flagship Edinburgh Gin is clean, fresh and spicy. In the mouth pine comes to the forefront with heathery scented notes following on. This is a well-balanced crisp gin with a gingery spiciness and laid-back citrus.

A number of interesting bottlings have also enhanced the now rather impressive portfolio. The Navy-strength Cannonball at 57.2% ABV is seriously punchy with bags of flavour. The Seaside Gin is made with locally foraged botanical from the Scottish shoreline such as seaweed, gorse flowers and scurvy grass (which sailors suffering from scurvy used to eat for Vitamin C).

They also produce an excellent range of gin liqueurs, including the much raved about Rhubarb and Ginger.

FOUR PILLARS RARE DRY GIN

The great early-21st-century gin craze has reached almost every corner of the globe and the Antipodes are no exception. Australia is experiencing an unprecedented explosion of small distillers making unique gins using a combination of classic and homegrown botanicals.

The Four Pillars Distillery in the wine-growing Yarra Valley near Melbourne was a pioneer of this trend when it was established in 2013. Based on an Australian grain spirit, the Four Pillars Rare recipe is the product of months of experimentation during which the botanicals were refined down to 10 – the usual suspects plus cardamom pods, lemon myrtle, Tasmanian pepper berry leaf, cinnamon, lavender, star anise and organic whole fresh oranges.

This mélange of Old and New World flavours has produced a genuinely fresh twist on the classic London Dry style. As you would expect, a blast of orange opens the door to an intriguing taste experiences, with the warmth of Tasmanian pepper berry leaf snuggling up to the soft citrus of lemon myrtle used here as an alternative to the more traditional lemon peel. With an ABV of 41.8% strong juniper ensures there is no doubt this is gin but gin with a relaxed Down Under beach attitude.

The Four Pillars portfolio has grown to include a Navy Strength Gin, Barrel Aged Gin, Spiced Negroni Gin, Australian Christmas

Gin, Modern Australian Gin and Bloody Shiraz Gin. The latter is particularly interesting as it is made by steeping whole locally grown Shiraz grapes in Rare Dry for eight weeks then pressing the fruit and adding more gin. Each year's vintage is slightly different and these limited-edition bottlings consistently sell out every year.

GLENDALOUGH WILD BOTANICAL GIN

Distilling in Ireland has a long and proud history and the Glendalough Distillery in Co. Wicklow was founded with the specific aim of reviving that heritage. Currently the distillery produces single-grain Irish whiskey, poitín and, of course, gin.

Because the emphasis here is so much on using botanicals that grow locally in the wild Wicklow Mountains, the company initially focused on producing a range of gins following the seasons. Building on this idea of local and seasonal provenance the focus is now on the core product: Glendalough Wild Botanical Gin. Working with local forager Geraldine Kavanagh, the heady recipe has evolved to include core gin botanicals plus liquorice root and bark, lemon, elderflower, red clover, yarrow, ox eye daisy, wild raspberry, blackberry leaves, wild rose, watermint, sweet woodruff, lemon balm, sweet cicely, lady's bedstraw and bell heather.

Produced on site in a magnificent 500l Arnold Holstein copper still, each run takes around 24 hours from maceration through to final distillation. This long slow process allows the more volatile floral and herbal elements of the recipe to become firmly embedded.

At 41% ABV, Glendalough opens up with juniper, citrus and pine. As the aromas develop one is presented with a gorgeous floral bouquet with gentle spice aromas. An intriguing gin that works well in all the classic serves and probably needs very little in the way of garnish, but I am told that mint and orange in a G and T makes it even more delicious.

A collaboration between chef Valentine Warner, drinks guru Nick Strangeway, drinks developer Cairbry Hill, estate owner Walter Riddell and distiller Chris Garden, Hepple Gin is made in a purpose-built distillery in the wilds of Northumberland.

Hepple uses 13 different botanicals including Douglas Fir, bog myrtle, lovage, blackcurrant leaf, blackcurrants, Amalfi lemons, fennel seeds, liquorice, orris root and three different types of juniper – Italian juniper, Macedonian juniper and green juniper grow locally on the Hepple estate.

That's not the only thing unusual about this gin. It's uniquely made through a combination of three different flavour extraction methods. These are: the traditional one of distilling with botanicals in a pot still, vacuum distillation in a glass still to capture the more delicate aromas of local botanicals such as the green juniper and lovage, and a specially designed high-pressure CO_2 extraction process to embed the flavours of the more pungent Macedonian juniper. The resulting three distillates are then blended together before being bottled at 45% ABV.

And is all this time and effort reflected in the final quality of the gin? Yes and double yes. Strongly juniper when first encountered on the nose, the gin then opens up to a complicated yet perfectly balanced combination of pine, fruit and woodiness wrapped in a great big duvet of lush herbaceousness. Hepple is a watchmaker's gin, one of the very best things to come out of the great gin revolution.

HERNÖ GIN

European nations have embraced the great gin revolution with gusto, nowhere more so than in the Nordic countries. The Hernö Distillery is located in Härnösand, a town on Sweden's remote eastern coast that is part of a UNESCO world heritage site. It's also believed to be the most northerly gin distillery in Europe (that could have changed by the time you're reading this however!)

The core Hernö range kicked off with Swedish Excellence, a London Dry-ish gin with a Scandi twist in the form of the addition of vanilla, handpicked lingonberries and local meadowsweet. The first impression is of forest-floor mossiness followed by fresh mountain pine with a vanilla sweetness. Bottled at three different strengths – 40.5% ABV, Export at 47% ABV and Navy at 57% ABV – these are exceptionally bold and flavoursome gins that probably work better in a Negroni than a G and T.

Hernö Old Tom at 43% ABV is very different in flavour. Made with local honey from MittBi less than 3km from the distillery, there's a pronounced sweetness with juniper firmly in the back seat.

In 2013 Hernö pioneered the idea of maturing gin in juniper wood with the launch of its Juniper Cask variant. Here fresh woodiness and pine combine to produce an intensely ginny gin that will appeal to all juniper fanatics. Hernö gins consistently win awards and are beloved of the global gin community.

Building a distillery on the remote Isle of Harris was the vision of long term Harris resident, Anderson Bakewell, a renowned American musicologist, who saw the opportunity to boost the local economy by creating a range of spirits that would embody the unique spirit of the island.

Fast forward to the opening of the distillery in 2015 with the tagline "The Social Distillery". To date The Hearach, a single-malt whisky, has been made and laid down to mature. Its first batch is limited to 1,916 bottles, one for every man, woman and child living on Harris at the time of bottling.

In the meantime there's a very good gin. A lot of thought has gone into it as the distillers wanted to incorporate flavours that reflected the unique terroir of the Western Isles. An ethno-botanist was hired to find a local, sustainable ingredient that would work as a gin botanical. After much searching it turned out to be sugar kelp, a type of seaweed that flourishes in underwater forests all around the island. It's hand-harvested by a local diver.

Sugar kelp and the other eight botanicals that make up the recipe, including liquorice root, cubeb berries, bitter orange peel and cassia bark, are placed in the still with a neutral grain spirit to infuse. The sugar kelp is then removed and the other botanicals distilled slowly in the traditional manner. At 45% ABV the first impression is of soft juniper with citrus zestiness. The flavours develop to contribute pleasant salty, vegetal notes with a definite tang of the sea. Suggested serve here is a G and T with Walter Gregor's Scottish tonic water, and a few drops of the distillery's own sugar kelp aromatic water plus a grapefruit garnish.

JAWBOX SMALL BATCH GIN

The brainchild of Belfast barman Gerry White, Jawbox Small Batch Gin is named after the famous Belfast sink, colloquially known as the "Jawbox", the heart of every Belfast home around which families would gather to share stories.

Made at the Echlinville Distillery on the beautiful Ards Peninsula in Kircubbin outside Belfast from barley that grows locally, it's another fine example of the growing trend for field-to-glass spirit production.

Jawbox describes itself as Ireland's only single-estate gin. Eleven botanicals make up the recipe majoring on the more unusual grains of paradise, liquorice root, cubebs, cardamom, cassia quills and locally foraged Black Mountain heather. A slow distillation in a traditional copper pot still ensures full extraction of these complex flavours. It is bottled at a sturdy 43% ABV.

On the nose, Jawbox makes a big impact with bold heathery juniper and pine, balanced with a gentle touch of sweet coriander and clean citrus, developing in the mouth to a more complex flavour profile with peppery, spicy notes.

The preferred Jawbox serve calls on another Belfast invention: ginger ale. Try it in a Gin Buck with 35ml Jawbox gin in an ice-filled glass, topped up with premium ginger ale and garnished with a wedge of lime.

y

It's always been a bit of a mystery why gin has traditionally never been big in Japan. My personal gin guru, Desmond Payne, says that it's because tonic water in Japan has always been poor with an even higher percentage of sickly sweet high fructose corn syrup than one finds in other countries for some strange reason. It's even more mysterious when one considers that the Japanese are a nation of people who appreciate fine spirits and Japanese distillers now make whisky to rival Scotch.

It's all rapidly changing however. First of all good-quality tonic waters are now widely available and the Japanese have discovered the delights of a properly made G and T. Secondly the launch of Japan's first ever artisan gin distillery in Kyoto in 2016 was major news. Owned by two UK-based drinks stalwarts, Marcin Miller and David Croll, the Kyoto Distillery has to date focused on the development of its flagship product: Ki No Bi (Beauty of the Seasons).

Master Distiller Alex Davies of the Kyoto Distillery uses a spirit base distilled from rice and has included specifically Japanese botanicals such as yellow yuzu, hinoki (cypress) wood chips, bamboo, gyokuro tea, and green sanshō (Japanese peppercorn) as well as juniper, orris and lemon peel. The botanicals in Ki No Bi are divided into six different categories: base, citrus, tea, herbal, spice and floral. Each category is separately steeped in rice spirit and then individually distilled before being blended together.

Once distilled Ki No Bi is reduced to 45.7% ABV using water from Fushimi, known for its purity. Clearly, someone with a total understanding of how flavour works has made this gin. Juniper is present but doesn't dominate, there's spice and lovely green herbal notes, just the right amount of citrus and very subtle hints of tea. All in all it's exceptionally smooth and well balanced, one of the few gins one could easily drink neat.

LIVERPOOL GIN

It seems extraordinary that it took until 2013 for the great port city of Liverpool to have its own gin again, especially given that in the 18th century Liverpool was a major distilling centre and a hub of international trade. The city's Vauxhall Distillery and the Bank Hall Distillery once produced vast amounts of grain spirit for whisky and also for rectification into gin. Indeed the Bank Hall Distillery, which closed down in the last century, was situated, most appropriately, on a road called Juniper Street.

Liverpool Gin is made at the Liverpool Organic Brewery near the former site of aforementioned Bank Hall and proudly carries the city's Liver Bird symbol on its bottle. Provenance is taken seriously here and all the botanicals, i.e. the classic ones plus liquorice, orange, cassia and cardamom and the base spirit used, are certified 100% organic.

On the nose there is juniper and sharp menthol, almost chloroform, aromas from liquorice and cassia. In the mouth there's an instant blast of citrus zestiness alongside green juniper and some soft, slightly musky spice notes.

At 43% ABV Liverpool is a big gin that shines in a G and T. The makers recommend using a chunk (can be frozen too) of watermelon as a garnish and it's robust enough to stand out in one of the new herb-heavy tonic waters such Lamb & Watt's Basil.

There are two other flavoured gins in the range, both made from organic ingredients. Liverpool Rose Petal is delightfully floral and fresh whilst Liverpool Valencian Orange, a limited-edition bottling, delivers a huge blast of refreshing orange citrus.

Liverpool: since 1207

LIVERPOOL GIN

ARTISANAL ORGANIC ENGLISH GIN

43%Vol Product of England 70cl℮

LUSSA GIN

The island of Jura off the west coast of Scotland is well known for its distilling expertise as it makes some of the best Scotch whisky in the world. Ever since three enterprising local women set up a small distillery on the Ardlussa Estate in the north of the island, gin is fast becoming the spirit this Hebridean paradise is most famous for. (Incidentally Ardlussa is right next door to Barnhill where George Orwell wrote his famous novel *Nineteen Eighty-Four*.)

Claire Fletcher, Alicia MacInnes and Georgina Kitching are nothing if not adventurous and many of the 15 botanicals that make up the Lussa Gin recipe are grown or gathered on the island. After juniper and coriander, the main ingredient is lemon thyme grown in poly tunnels and outdoors with many island neighbours growing it too in exchange for gin. The sea lettuce is harvested by boat and they handpick ground elder, Scots pine needles, bog myrtle, honeysuckle flowers, rosehips, watermint, lime tree flowers and elderflower through the growing season. Roses are a big part of the botanical mix and they cultivate particularly highly scented varieties in the Ardlussa garden.

Unusually all the botanicals are frozen before distillation in order to retain more of the aromatic oils. The botanicals are then macerated overnight before a gentle distillation aided by a water bath.

Bottled at 42% ABV Lussa Gin is packed with fragrant, earthy, herbaceous flavours with rose and lemon thyme prominent. A top tip is to go the whole floral route and enjoy it with Fentiman's Rose Lemonade in an easy-to-make long drink.

MASONS DRY YORKSHIRE GIN

Founded by gin lovers Karl and Catherine Mason, who knew enough about gin to make a spirit to appeal to their own very specialized taste, Masons Yorkshire Gin is made in the small market town of Bedale. In fact it seems the Masons have singlehandedly revived the tradition of distilling in Yorkshire.

The recipe features almond oil, fennel, cardamom, bay leaf, Szechuan pepper and lemon, orange and lime zests. So, in many ways Masons Dry is a very classic juniper-led gin with lovely spice and citrus notes.

In 2015 the original Masons Yorkshire Gin was boosted with the arrival of two sister expressions – Yorkshire Gin Lavender Edition and Yorkshire Gin Tea Edition. All three gins are bottled at 42% ABV and promote their use of Harrogate water to reduce bottling strength. Given that a terrifyingly large proportion of the gin in your bottle is water, that's reassuring.

Using tea as a botanical in gin has become a bit of a thing. Pioneered by Beefeater in the very splendid Beefeater 24, it doesn't always work. In fact one could safely draw a veil over the Heston Blumenthal Earl Grey and Lemon experiment – a rare miss for that master of flavour. The Yorkshire Tea edition is very different. On the nose dark, tannin notes make an instant impression and mix perfectly with piney juniper and the softer spice flavours of cardamom and fennel. On tasting with water the flavours become more perfumed but remain crisp and refreshing as the citrus blast kicks in.

The Oro Gin Distilling Company in the small village of Dalton in Dumfriesshire is the latest addition to the booming Scottish gin scene.

It's a family-owned venture headed up by Ray Clynick, a scientist who is also a graduate of the prestigious Heriot Watt International Centre for Brewing and Distilling. His mission is to create the perfect gin based on scientific principles and a thorough understanding of how different flavour compounds interact with each other. After months of experimentation the botanicals selected for the flagship Oro and Oro V recipes are a combination of classic gin botanicals and the more rarely used cassia bark, Malabar cardamom, pink peppercorns and lemongrass. There's also one other signature botanical that I am assured will forever remain secret.

The botanicals are macerated for 24 hours and then distilled in copper using the one-shot method. Such is the precision here that even the rectifying column through which the gin vapour passes after distillation to return to liquid is also made of copper in order to achieve an even cleaner, fresher taste.

Both gins are bottled 43% ABV. Oro standard is an extremely well-balanced gin with fresh, green juniper acting as a bright

introduction to subtler honeyed elements with lingering leather notes. I'm thinking gorse or vanilla but the secret remains secret. Oro V is super floral thanks to the addition of lavender and bumped-up orris with its Parma Violet fragrance. It's highly aromatic with enough differentiation from the other Oro to provide a real choice. Apparently both expressions scored equally well in preliminary tastings so the decision was made to launch them at the same time.

At the heart of the Distillery is The Lab, a hub of innovation that specializes in limited-edition bottlings as well as specialities like aged gin and fruit gins. The Dalton Distillery also has a charming restaurant and bar and runs a series of Distillery Tours that can be pre-booked (*see Gin Places* on page 191).

Oxford Dry Gin is made at The Oxford Artisan Distillery (TOAD), Oxford's first distillery. It's another terrific example of creating a field-to-glass spirit.

Founder Tom Nicholson and master distiller Cory Mason make their grain spirit from scratch at the distillery. Such is their passion for authenticity that they use ancient varieties of "land race" cereals grown locally by John Letts, an archaeo-botanist. These land race grains are genetically diverse and each plant in the field is different, creating a crop that is more vigorous, healthy and hardy without the need for chemicals.

Local provenance is a strong theme that continues with many of the botanicals used in the Oxford Dry recipe handpicked from the Oxford Botanic Garden nearby. The more exotic ones are sourced sustainably from organic growers whenever possible. Indeed TOAD's Cory Mason claims to know exactly where every single ingredient in his gin comes from. And a partnership with the Oxford Botanic Garden, Britain's oldest teaching garden, will allow for more experimentation based on the garden's extensive historical plant archive.

Bottled at a very decent 46% ABV, on the nose Oxford Dry is as clean as a whistle, fresh and almost medicinally juniper. In the mouth juniper, coriander and citrus combine to create a full, well-rounded palate. There's sweetness too at the tip of the tongue and a hint of warm spiciness reminiscent of cinnamon and cardamom. A long lush finish completes the experience.

In addition to gin, the TOAD Distillery also makes absinthe, vodka and rye whiskey all according to the field-to-bottle ethos.

Pickering's Gin is a prime example of the artisan distilling movement that is sweeping the UK. It's made in Edinburgh by two self-confessed gin nuts at the arts complex Summerhall, formerly the University's Veterinary School aka the Dick Vet. Marcus Pickering and partner Matt Gammell have transformed what were once the Vet School's dog kennels into a small but perfectly formed distillery that is the first new legal distillery in the city for almost 200 years. Cleverly they've also run a line into Summerhall's bar, the Royal Dick, so that Pickering's is available there on tap.

Bottled at 42% ABV Pickering's has nine botanicals including cardamom, fennel, anise, lemon, lime and cloves. It's loosely based on an old colonial Raj recipe handed down to founder Marcus Pickering's family.

Astonishingly for gin novices, Pickering and Gammell have actually invented a unique "bain-marie" system to provide a more consistent heat to the still. Slow, immersive heat gently embeds the botanical flavours in the spirit capturing the fresh citrus notes as well as the more earthy spice aromas. The result is a gin that has the clean fresh pine notes of juniper at its heart and is strongly aromatic in the mouth with hints of liquorice and warm spice. The crisp dry finish is characterized by a lingering lavender-like softness. It's a true gin-lover's gin.

Pickering's Navy is bottled at 57.1 ABV whilst Pickering's Original 1947 is an even more faithful rendition of the recipe that inspired the whole project with extra cloves and more curry-type spice flavours making their presence felt. There's also a range of oak-aged gins rather imaginatively matured in five different types of whisky cask from the five different Scottish whisky regions.

However strange as it may seem the Pickering's name is now known all over the world for their invention of Christmas baubles filled with gin. No matter how many they make each year they always sell out.

There is a growing trend for bartenders to produce their own spirits with Ford's Gin and Hernö Gin springing to mind. And why not? It makes sense: who better than an experienced bartender knows what flavours work best in cocktails and what is precisely required from a spirit? Porter's Gin is a labour of love created by two of the UK's leading bartenders Ben Iravani and Alex Lawrence and friend/businessman Josh Rennie.

Porter's is made with an unusual combination of traditional botanicals, less used botanicals such as almond, liquorice, pink peppercorns and one that was completely new to me called Buddha's Hand, a rare and curious form of citrus that looks like a bunch of fingers painted by Modigliani during a yellow period. Distilling methods are unconventional too, employing a combination of traditional pot still and cold distillation techniques. The main body of the gin, i.e. juniper, coriander seed, angelica, liquorice, almond, lemon peel, orange peel and cinnamon, is made by G & J Distillers at the Greenall's Distillery in Warrington. This is then transported to Porter's tiny distillery in Aberdeen where it is blended with a distillate made on a small glass Rotovap from pink peppercorn, cassia and Buddha's Hand. Porter's is then bottled at 41.5% ABV.

Obviously no one in their right mind would choose such a complicated process, but years of experimentation, both with flavour and how to best extract it, underpin the search for quality here so it's gratifying to see that Porter's is not your average gin. It's not a London Dry in terms of production nor does it aspire to be, proudly announcing its Aberdeen location, but it is exceptionally classy with a delightful juniper forward character, nice warming spice notes and multi-layered citrus.

SHETLAND REEL GIN

Saxa Vord Distillery on Unst in the Shetlands is the most northerly distillery in the whole of the UK. Here, in what was once an RAF base, the distillery makes single-malt whisky and, whilst waiting for it to mature, has embarked on an interesting gin adventure that puts its location's unique natural environment centre stage.

Shetland Reel Gin is made with eight botanicals with its signature botanical being apple mint grown and harvested on the island. Launched to great acclaim in 2015, the gin has won numerous awards. No wonder, its juniper character and spicy sweetness with a citrus tang make it the perfect gin for a host of citrusy fruity gin cocktails. The distillery has also been quick to capitalize on the flexibility that small batch distilling provides and their gin family has expanded to include Shetland Reel Ocean Scent made with native bladderwrack seaweed and Shetland Simmer to celebrate the endless summer nights of this far outpost of the northern hemisphere.

There's also an annual series of limited-edition gins timed to coincide with Up Helly Aa, Shetland's famous January fire festival, a time when the whole population turns out to commemorate the islands' Viking heritage.

SILENT POOL GIN

There is a real Silent Pool, a local beauty spot near Guildford in the Surrey Hills that is reputedly haunted. On its banks, in what was once an old barn, a group of enthusiastic distillers now make magic on a daily basis.

Silent Pool Gin is made with 24 botanicals, including two different types of juniper, with many ingredients sourced locally. To preserve these flavours intact the distillery team employs a variety of distilling methods combing maceration, infusion and vapour distillation.

The more traditional botanicals – Bosnian juniper, cassia bark, coriander seed, green cardamom, angelica root, bitter orange peel, bergamot, cubeb berries, orris root, Grains of Paradise and honey – are steeped for 24 hours and distilled in the conventional way. More volatile elements such as lavender, kaffir lime leaves, chamomile, rose, linden flowers, and elderflower are infused in a sort of giant tea-bag and their oils added to the still. Fresh orange, fresh lime, pear, Macedonian juniper and angelica root are placed in a basket at the top of the still where they add their flavours to the botanical rich vapour as it passes through.

Complicated yes but clearly a lot of thought has gone into maximizing the flavour extraction possible from such a diverse array of ingredients. On tasting there's no question there's a lot going on here. On the nose green juniper and fresh floral aromas are to the fore. In the mouth juniper becomes more intense and, as the flavours develop, a pronounced almost jasmine-like fragrance emerges. There's a bit of sweetness too and a particularly nice aromatic dryness at the back of the throat. At 43% ABV Silent Pool is a complex gin that delivers on every front. Recommended serve is with a handful of ice and just a dash of tonic.

THE LAKES GIN

The Lake District does not immediately spring to mind as a location for a state-of-the-art distillery making not just gin but also single-malt and blended whiskies, and vodka. But former whisky entrepreneur Paul Currie clearly knows what he is doing. Opened in December 2014, the Lakes Distillery is housed in a beautiful restored Victorian cattle farm with an award-winning Michelin star restaurant on-site. The Lakes Gin is made with local botanicals foraged on the fells, including heather, bilberry, hawthorn, meadowsweet and the native Cumbrian juniper as well as cassia bark and other exotics. Bottled at 43.7% ABV, this is a gin packed with flavour. Citrus and juniper predominate with floral notes and a laid-back berry sweetness. G and T would be the obvious choice as the juniper character is robust enough to shine. A Collins with a garnish of blackberries would also work well.

VERDANT DRY GIN

Based in the former engine house of one of Dundee's old jute mills, Verdant Spirits is the first and only distillery in the city for almost 200 years. Building on the heritage of the city's industrial and entrepreneurial past, founder Andrew McKenzie celebrated the Dundonian ethos of innovation with the installation of one of the new generation of stills – a 500-litre iStill. It's not the prettiest piece of equipment but Verdant believes it does the best possible job for the production of the best possible craft spirits.

Proof of the pudding is that barely were Verdant's distillery doors open than its flagship product, Verdant Dry Gin, was crowned "Gin of the Year" at the 2017 Scottish Gin Awards, against some pretty stiff competition too.

In many ways Verdant Dry Gin is a very classic London Dry Gin, refreshing really nowadays when one is inundated with weird and wonderful botanical combinations (not all of which work). Verdant keeps it simple – juniper, coriander seed, lemon peel, cassia bark, angelica, green cardamom, grains of paradise and liquorice. These traditional spices, berries and herbs also give the nod to Dundee's important trading history and reflect the routes once sailed by Scottish ships to and from its port.

On the nose Verdant is very clean, with understated yet clearly present juniper. In the mouth there is initially an almost antiseptic blast of fresh, camphor-like juniper with gentle citrus notes underpinned by laid-back peppery spice. Sweetness on the tip of the tongue indicates the presence of liquorice.

With a bottling strength of 43% ABV this an exceptionally well-balanced gin with the character to shine in all the signature gin drinks, but I can't help but feel it makes the most magnificent Martini.

VIDDA TØRR GIN

Vidda Tørr Gin is a relatively new offering from Norway where gin has been growing in popularity for some years. The name translates as "mountain plateau dry" and says it all really. This is a spirit that is firmly within the British Dry style but is made with botanicals foraged in the Norwegian wilderness. The philosophy here was to create a gin that would capture the essence of the pristine Norwegian mountain landscape and embody the Norwegian passion for foraging (*nyttevekst*) that is such a crucial part of the Scandinavian way of life.

The final recipe consists of juniper, heather, yarrow, chamomile flower, bilberry, angelica, meadowsweet, sorrel, calamus, elderflower and pine shoots. Most of these botanicals are picked locally during the short but intense northern growing season. The mix is steeped overnight in the still in a neutral base spirit before distillation starts. When the run is complete and the spirit collected, it is then rested for around two weeks to allow the flavours to integrate.

At 43% ABV Vidda Tørr is a gin that the Vikings might have drunk on their way to a spot of marauding. Pine-rich juniper is to the fore but there are also earthy forest floor aromas in here too. These combine with floral, green notes from elderflower and meadowsweet to make for an invigorating experience.

Try it with tonic garnished with a chunk of fresh pink grapefruit, or on its own.

SPECIALITY GINS

One reason for the success of gin in recent years is that distillers have been proactive in expanding the boundaries of gin beyond the traditional, aromatic, juniper-dominant taste profile. Old Tom Gin, the sweet style of gin popular in the 19th century, has made a comeback. Distillers experiment with aged gins using different types of casks to create gins that are more like fine malt whiskies.

The variety of fruits now used to flavour gin is almost bewildering and ranges from the very traditional sloe gin to a new spit-roasted pineapple-flavoured gin. In many ways it's a return to the past where most distillers made a huge variety of different types of gin as contemporary price lists show. There's even been an upsurge of interest in gin's ancestor Dutch genever with many traditional brands finding new audiences.

....

Some say the trend for ageing gin in wood is a return to the authenticity of the gin of the 19th century when it was stored and transported in wooden barrels. This argument is not particularly convincing because actually the wood used to make storage barrels was very old wood that had been used many times and would not have imparted further flavour. Secondly the implication that somehow the gin of the Victorian gin palace was inherently better than modern gin is just not realistic. In fact the opposite is true: modern distilling techniques and stricter quality controls mean that we now live in a golden age of gin production. That said however, if the aim is purely to bring something new to the party in terms of flavour, aged gins certainly do the trick. They also expand our drinking repertoires to include gin as a *digestif* akin to a fine malt whisky or venerable old rum. And, I can't help but feel that, since most distillers just love playing around with flavour, the possibilities of cask ageing are just irresistible.

Aged gins are usually fairly limited-edition bottlings hence more likely to be available from specialist retailers. Some have been covered in the Brand Directory above and others worth a special mention are:

Burroughs Reserve: created by Master Distiller Desmond Payne from an ancient recipe devised by founder James Burrough, the spirit is uniquely rested in Jean de Lillet oak barrels.

Citadelle Réserve: aged for six months in oak, it has a fuller juniper taste with a slight oakiness and is bottled at 44% ABV.

Hayman's 1850 Reserve: distilled to a recipe from 1850 and rested for three to four weeks in Scotch whisky barrels.

Caorunn Speyside Aged GinL matured in whisky barrels from Speyside and bottled at 48% ABV.

Hernö Juniper Cask: aged in barrels made from wood and bottled at 47% ABV.

BANANA GIN

....

Banana gin is not a gin at all; it's the generic name for strong spirits in many parts of West Africa. This is a hangover from the shameful trading habits of the 18th century when the Dutch and English used genever and gin as a component of the 'triangular trade'. Their ships took goods, including spirits, to Africa, exchanged them for slaves – who were transported to the Caribbean and the Americas – and there loaded up with sugar and tobacco which they brought back home. To this day original stone genever bottles are regularly dug up in remote parts of West Africa, a reminder of this practice. These "gins" are essentially fruit schnapps-type spirits usually made from bananas, hence the name. They are principally used for ritual purposes, poured out on to the ground for example, as a ceremonial offering. Frankly this is the best thing to do with them.

DUTCH GENEVER

There are three styles of genever – oude, jonge and korenwijn – and there are aged and unaged varieties. Under European law, each style of genever must contain different minimum percentages of maltwine (a grain spirit with a fiery taste and a distinctive spirity character), botanicals and sugar, and be bottled at different alcoholic strengths. This is how it works:

OUDE GENEVER is the traditional genever, similar in taste to the original English Genevas. It must contain a minimum of 15% maltwine, no more than 20 grammes of sugar per litre and be bottled at at least 35% ABV. It does not have to be aged but often is. It also often has far higher percentages of maltwine than required.

JONGE GENEVER was developed in the 1950s in response to the demand for a more mixable, lighter-flavoured spirit. It is bottled at a minimum of 35% ABV and contains a maximum of 15% maltwine and no more than 10 grammes of sugar per litre. If the label mentions *graanjenever* [grain genever], then the base spirit is 100% grain. Jonge genever is colourless and very light on the palate.

The terms "oude" [old] and "jonge" [young] are confusing as one naturally thinks of aged and unaged. But in this case, they refer to "old style" and "new style".

KORENWIJN (or corenwyn) contains a minimum of 51% maltwine so it has a very malty, full-bodied taste. It must be at least 38% ABV and contain no more than 20 grammes of sugar per litre. Korenwijn is quite rare outside the Benelux countries but if you come across it, it's definitely worth a try. It's the Dutch equivalent of single-malt whisky. Drink it ice-cold on its own, or try it mixed in an Old-Fashioned.

Although Dutch genever is no longer widely drunk except in Dutch "brown cafes", there are still over 200 brands on the market, including fruit-flavoured ones. Many are very localized – made locally and sold in the local pub. The market is dominated by 15 major producers, of whom the largest are De Kuypers, Bols and Heineken.

FRUIT GINS

In the 19th century all the traditional distillers made a vast range of fruit-flavoured gins – orange, lemon, ginger, lovage, raspberry, damson, blackcurrant, greengage and sloe amongst them. Although many commercially produced fruit gins disappeared in the 1950s, they are back, and today one sees a large array of fruit gins available especially from smaller rural producers.

Sloe gin never went away. Described as a "British liqueur", it's made by steeping wild sloe berries, the fruit of the blackthorn tree, in gin and allowing the flavours to marry. Once the favourite drink of prim Victorian ladies and the tweed-clad, sloe gin has made the leap from the hip flasks of the hunting, shooting and fishing set to the backs of the most stylish bars. There's now a raft of new ways of drinking sloe gin in cocktails and long drinks that tie in with the fashion for drinking seasonally, using locally sourced ingredients. Try it with English apple juice, garnished with an apple slice. Or add 25ml of sloe gin to Champagne or sparkling wine for an apéritif that not only tastes great but also looks very pretty. Sloe gin is also delicious on its own: an excellent alternative to brandy or port as an after-dinner drink.

Both Gordon's and Plymouth make sloe gin. Another traditional brand, Hawker's Sloe Gin, has come back into production and many farm shops have also got in on the act, producing excellent sloe gins. However, sloe gin is easy to make at home.

Gather your sloe berries in the autumn after the first frosts. Fill a gin bottle halfway with sloes, add two inches of caster sugar and top up with full-strength gin. Leave for several weeks to mature. Shake the bottle every now and again, if you remember, and there it is.

FRUIT CUPS

The first and the original Pimm's No. 1 Fruit Cup was invented by James Pimm in London in 1840. He owned a chain of restaurants all over the City and made a proto-alcopop by blending gin with liqueurs, herbs and spices that he then sold to his customers in pint tankards. In 1859, he started bottling it for sale to other bars and restaurants. The company was sold to Sir Horatio Davis, a city entrepreneur, who developed an export trade for Pimm's. One of the first-recorded shipments was to the famous Galle Face Hotel in Colombo, Sri Lanka. Pimm's was also sent up the Nile, in 1898, to the forces at Khartoum and Omdurman in the Sudan.

Other Pimm's cups were introduced, based on Scotch (No. 2), brandy (No. 3), rum (No. 4), rye whisky (No. 5) and vodka (No. 6). But the first sip of the gin-based Pimm's No. 1 is still the harbinger of English summer.

GINEBRA SAN MIGUEL

Ginebra San Miguel is made in the Philippines and it is by far the biggest-selling gin brand in the world. If you ever come across it, you will wonder why: it tastes of kerosene flavoured with pine lavatory cleaner. It's bottled at 40% in small beer bottles and its massive sales reflect the fact that, outside the Muslim areas in the south, Filipino social life revolves around drinking San Miguel. Since the Philippines is one of the most populous countries in the world it's easy to see how they get through so much.

DRINKING
GIN

There are hundreds of ways to drink gin, ranging from the greatest cocktail of all time, the Dry Martini, to the *kopstet* (literally a blow to the head) – the Dutch habit of drinking genever with a half pint of lager and considered the ultimate hangover cure. In reality, the way most people encounter gin is via a Gin and Tonic.

HISTORY IN A GLASS

Gin and tonic water is one of those combinations that seem made for each other, the clean taste of the gin enhancing the aromatic bitterness of the tonic in a drink that is subtle, refreshing and quintessentially British. And, like other well-loved institutions – tea, suburban bungalows, pyjamas and kedgeree – Gin and Tonic owes its existence to the British presence in India.

Like gin, tonic water began life as a medicine. Its principal flavour is derived from quinine, which in turn is derived from the bark of a magical tree, *cinchona officinalis*, that grew in South America. In the 16th century Spanish colonialists found native healers using this bark as a cure for fever, particularly malaria, and began using it themselves calling it cinchona or Jesuit's Bark. Quinine is a wonder drug in that it not only calms the fever and shivering associated with malaria but also kills the parasite that causes the disease so it can be used as both a cure and a preventative treatment. In fact it is one of the most effective drugs ever known to man – Winston Churchill once attributed it with saving "more Englishmen's lives, and minds, than all the doctors in the Empire".

Spanish Jesuit missionaries sent supplies back home to headquarters in Rome, a city particularly prone to outbreaks of malaria because of its marshy terrain. Jesuits promoted the use of the new wonder drug – hence the term Jesuit's Bark – but unfortunately that caused it to be viewed with the utmost suspicion by northern European Protestant nations who particularly hated the Jesuits. Doctors in Holland, Germany and England actively rejected the idea of any cure coming from this source.

The fame of Jesuit's Bark spread when Charles II of England was cured of malaria by a notorious quack, Robert Talbot, using the Jesuit's Bark powder mixed with wine. Charles appointed Talbot his personal physician and sent him to the French court where he proceeded to cure the king of France's son too. Talbot, despite his lack of medical training, managed to do what no one else had, and that is to understand how the bark should be administered. Crucially he discovered that quinine alkaloids were highly soluble in alcohol – so wine, not water, was the ideal medium for extracting them.

By the end of the 17th century cinchona bark was widely accepted throughout Europe as a treatment for malaria. But it was wildly expensive and varied hugely in quality, with some bark having no medicinal effect at all. Nobody knew why this was so. Over the next 150 years many expeditions were sent secretly to South America to find out more about the cinchona tree.

Slowly there developed a scientific understanding of how quinine worked, which species of tree was the best source, how it could be processed efficiently and what the correct dosages were.

By the end of the 18th century the British Navy was issuing its sailors with wine-based quinine tonics. In the 1840s British soldiers and colonials in India were using 700 tons of cinchona bark every year and in 1848 quinine extracts were added to the military and naval daily rum ration. For countries with far-flung empires, quinine was a vital necessity. The race was on to break the Spanish monopoly on the precious bark and secure their own sources.

In the 1850s British and Dutch explorers began to smuggle seeds out of Latin America and planted cinchona trees in their tropical colonies – the British in India and Ceylon (now Sri Lanka). Unfortunately they did not produce the quality of quinine necessary. Finally the Dutch successfully established plantations in Java with seeds taken from Bolivia and these did produce the required standard of quinine. By 1918 the Dutch controlled the world's supply.

In British India the bitter flavour of the daily dose of quinine was made palatable by adding sugar and diluting the mixture with soda water. And here's where the other half of the perfect combination comes into play. The British had always used gin as trade goods in India. Gin was very much part of the British way of life in the Raj, part memory of "home" and all things British, part consolation, part indulgence. It wasn't long before someone had the bright idea that gin would enliven the quinine mixture. And so the perfect sundowner was born.

Returning expats brought the taste for this exotic, bitter drink home with them. Surprisingly, because one tends to think of proprietary bottled drinks as modern, commercial production of what were called "Tonic Brewed Drinks" began as long ago as the mid-19th century. In 1858, Erasmus Bond patented "an improved aerated tonic liquid" specifying the use of quinine and other flavouring agents including bitter orange. Soon there were many brands of tonic water on the market with Schweppes adding Indian tonic water to its range in the 1870s.

The Dutch dominated the quinine trade until the Second World War when the Japanese occupied Java. The resulting shortage of quinine fuelled the drive to develop a synthetic version of the alkaloid. By 1944 scientists had synthesized quinine and pharmaceutical companies were able to produce various quinine-based drugs. At the same time plantations of natural cinchona were successfully established in parts of Africa.

Most modern commercially produced tonic waters are based on synthetic quinine and hence taste quite different to the original Indian tonic water, particularly in the US where tonic water tends to be much sweeter and often contains the dreaded high fructose corn syrup. There's been a bit of a backlash against this and over the past few years many excellent authentic tonic waters that do contain natural quinine and, like the original tonic waters, other botanical ingredients, have come on to the market. In the UK the best are Fentimans, Fever-Tree, Bramley & Gage and Waitrose own brand.

RIGHT: *Fever-Tree Tonic Water is one of the new wave of premium mixers that uses natural quinine grown in Africa and other natural botanical ingredients.*

GIN AND TONIC

The Gin and Tonic is a great British invention that has now taken over the world. The USA and Japan were amongst the last countries to fall under its spell mostly because in both places the tonic water left a lot to be desired. However Spain is GinTonic heaven and, throughout the rest of Continental Europe, the Gin and Tonic is pretty much the gin signature serve.

A properly made Gin and Tonic is one of life's great pleasures. And although it's simple to make, use a few basic rules and one ends up with a drink that approaches perfection.

- Always use a good-quality gin.
- Use a single-serve bottle or can of tonic water.
- Take a tall glass with a heavy bottom. Fill it with ice (at least four large cubes) and add a generous measure of gin. Pour in enough tonic to fill the glass. What you're aiming for is just over double the amount of tonic to gin.
- Add a freshly cut wedge of lemon, lime or grapefruit and rub it around the rim of the glass first. Or with some very citrusy gins you can skip the extra citrus. Stir gently with a teaspoon or a cocktail stirrer.

The point about a Gin and Tonic is that it is the perfect early-evening drink. In fact the same is true of all gin-based drinks. They allow one to pass those potentially anxious hours between work and dinner at peace with the world and with oneself. Partly this is physiological – of all the common liquors gin gives the quickest lift. Partly it is psychological – gin has been associated with the hours of ease at the end of the day for a century or more.

Strange as it may seem, some people claim not to like gin. The truth is they probably don't like the taste of tonic water, which can be a Marmite-style "love it or loathe it" flavour. No problem: other mixers that work well in gin are cranberry juice, ginger ale, elderflower tonics, natural lemonade and even Appletiser. And, not to be forgotten, bitter lemon, a mixer that was common 50 years ago but has slightly fallen out of fashion. Commercial bitter lemon is tonic water with the addition of lemon juice and peel, and whilst Schweppes is the standard there are now boutique versions available from smaller producers like Fever-Tree and Fentimans.

THE DRY MARTINI

Only one thing can be said about the Dry Martini without venturing into a minefield: it is American, and, as the humorist H. L. Mencken said, "the only American invention as perfect as the sonnet". There are many conflicting stories concerning its origins. The most credible theory is proposed by drinks historians Anastasia Miller and Jared Brown who date the popularity of the mix of gin and dry (aka white) vermouth to the turn of the 20th century when the Italian Martini company was promoting heavily its new "Extra Dry Vermouth". It seems more than likely therefore that the drink took its name from the brand.

There is a fashion for calling any drink served in a Martini glass a Dry Martini. Ignore it. A proper Dry Martini is made with premium gin and French vermouth. There has always been much argument as to the correct way to make it. At one end of the divide are those who advocate a standard 4:1 gin-to-vermouth ratio. At the other are Martini aficionados like the filmmaker Luis Buñuel who advised "simply allowing a ray of sunlight to shine through a bottle of Noilly Prat before it hits the bottle of gin". Winston Churchill apparently just bowed in the direction of France as he measured his Plymouth Gin into a glass with an olive.

One hesitates to stick one's head over the parapet but what should be considered is, at what point is the Dry Martini still a cocktail and not just a glass of cold neat gin with a spray of lemon juice? For my money that point is reached when it's made the "in and out" way:

Into a cold metal shaker filled with ice pour one tablespoon of dry vermouth to coat the ice. Strain off the excess vermouth and pour in 210 ml of gin. Stir until ice-cold, and then strain into two cold cocktail glasses. Either zest the oil from two strips of lemon peel over each glass or garnish each drink with a single olive. A small, pickled cocktail onion makes it a Gibson. Notice the Martini here is stirred not shaken: science tells us to shake a drink when you want it colder and slightly more diluted, stir when you want more flavour.

There are variations of the Dry Martini that still preserve the integrity of the recipe. The Smoky Martini for example adds a spoonful of malt whisky floated over the top, the Dirty Martini a splash of olive brine. The Cajun Martini mixes gin infused with jalapeno chillies with dry vermouth and a pepper garnish.

The other main ingredient of the Martini is vermouth – from the German "wermut", the name of its principal flavouring, wormwood. Vermouth is white wine, blended, fortified and made aromatic through the addition of macerated herbs and spices, chiefly the flowers of wormwood (its leaves are used to make absinthe). There are three kinds of vermouth: Italian such as Martini & Rossi and Cinzano; Savoie; and southern French, typically Noilly Prat that is the best for Dry Martinis.

Ask for a Dry Martini in a bar and the bartender will practically hug you as mixing the drink is the ultimate test of cocktail craft and everyone has his or her own particular trick. It's also a bit of a test of drinking skill and should be approached with caution. As the old joke goes, "the Martini is like a woman's breasts because one is not enough and three's too many". Or, as Dorothy Parker put it:

"I like to have a Martini
Two at the very most
After three I'm under the table
After four I'm under the host"

THE COLLINS FAMILY

Of all gin long drinks the Collins is the most versatile and its basic combination of gin, sugar syrup, lemon juice and soda water can be played around with endlessly to reflect the taste profiles of different gins and to accommodate seasonal flavours. The beauty of the Collins is that its ingredients are simple and found in every kitchen. It's also a good alternative for those who find the taste of tonic water overpowering.

BELOW: *The Tom Collins cocktail is easy to create and its history can be traced back to "Professor" Jerry Thomas in the 1870s.*

TOM COLLINS

50 ml gin
Juice of half a lemon
100 ml soda water
2 tsp caster sugar
Wedge of fresh lemon

Add the lemon juice and sugar to a tall glass and stir until the sugar has dissolved. Add the gin then fill the glass with ice and stir. Top up with soda water and stir carefully once more. Garnish with one fresh lemon wedge.

Making sugar syrup, which many classic cocktail recipes call for, is easy. In a saucepan combine 250g caster sugar with 250 ml water. Bring to the boil, stirring, until sugar has dissolved. Allow to cool. Or if time is short just dissolve two teaspoons of caster sugar in two teaspoons of water.

CRIMSON FIZZ

50 ml gin
1 tablespoon sugar syrup
6 strawberries

Crush the strawberries and shake with the gin and sugar syrup for several minutes, then strain into a cold tall glass. Fizz up with bottled soda water, stirring continuously as water is added. The point of this drink is that it should be served foaming.

ELDERFLOWER COLLINS

50 ml gin
50 ml lemon juice
12.5 ml elderflower cordial
12.5 ml shot sugar syrup

Build in the glass, stirring well. Fizz up with bottled soda water, stirring continuously as water is added. Add ice. Delicious on a summer's day.

The Gin Rickey is first cousin to a Collins but is made with fresh lime juice rather than lemon juice and with no sugar. It can be traced to Shoemakers Restaurant in Washington where a bartender invented the drink in the early years of the 20th century. The first person to try it was a Colonel Jim Rickey, hence the name.

BELOW: *The peach and elderflower Collins is just part of the Collins family of cocktails.*

PEACH AND ELDERFLOWER COLLINS

50 ml gin
25 ml freshly squeezed lemon juice
15 ml elderflower cordial
One third of a fresh white peach, diced or
*   20 ml of good-quality white peach puree*
50 ml soda water

Muddle the diced white peach in the bottom of a clean highball glass. Add the fresh lemon juice, elderflower cordial and gin. Stir well. Add plenty of cubed ice. Stir again. Top with soda water then stir for a final time to chill and combine all of the ingredients. Garnish with a clear straw and a wedge of white peach.

RIGHT: *Pink Gin.*
Pinkers is the classic
gin drink that British
expats introduced to
the rest of the world.

PINK GIN

"Pinkers" – as it is known amongst sailors – is a very British drink that came into being courtesy of the Royal Navy. A navy ship's surgeon first used a combination of Angostura bitters, gin and a splash of water as a cure for seasickness during long sea voyages and the drink caught on. In former British colonies Pink Gin was known as Gin Pahit (Pahit means bitter in Malay) and the addition of tiny onions marinated in chilli makes it a Gin Piaj. Whatever its name, drinking this drink once instantly identified you as a navy man or a colonial. It's not a drink for the faint-hearted.

2 dashes Angostura bitters
1 part gin
1 part water

Swirl several drops of Angostura bitters around in a short glass. Shake out the residue and add the gin and water. No ice. Remember: it's British.

THE GIMLET

The super-simple combination of gin and Rose's Lime Juice also has a strong connection to the Royal Navy and dates back to 1867 when Lachlan Rose, a Scottish chandler based in Edinburgh, came up with a formula to preserve citrus fruit juice without using alcohol. It was desperately needed because scurvy, caused by a deficiency of vitamin C, was still a major danger for sailors on long sea voyages. With superb timing, that same year a law required all vessels, Royal Navy and Merchant, to carry limes, not lemons, to be given daily to the crews. This led to the remarkable success of Rose's Lime Juice and along the way resulted in British sailors being called "limeys".

Dr Gimlette, a British naval surgeon, reputedly invented the drink that was then named after him. Here's the recipe:

1 part gin
1 part Rose's Lime Juice (it doesn't work with fresh lime juice)

Pour ingredients into a mixing glass three-quarters filled with ice cubes. Stir until ice-cold. Strain into a chilled Martini glass. Garnish with a slice of lime peel.

LEFT: *Another simple gin cocktail is the Gimlet; just gin and lime juice, but not freshly squeezed lime.*

OTHER CLASSIC COCKTAILS

THE WHITE LADY

Invented in the 1920s by Scottish bartender Harry MacElhone, initially at Ciro's. Later perfected at the famous Harry's New York Bar in Paris in 1929.

50 ml gin
19 ml Cointreau
19 ml freshly squeezed lemon juice
6 ml sugar syrup
1/2 egg white

Shake with ice, strain into a chilled Martini glass and garnish with a lemon twist.

For a Clover Club add 25 ml of raspberry syrup.

THE NEGRONI

The Negroni is the most perfect gin aperitif, one that real gin-lovers love. It's also a drink whose provenance can be traced to a specific time and place. Imagine the scene: the Bar Casoni in Florence, circa 1920, where patrons are enjoying their Americanos, a drink made with Campari, sweet vermouth and soda water, named thus because of pro-American feelings after World War I. But one regular had his own ideas: every day, Count Camillo Negroni ordered his Americano to be made with gin and without soda water. Soon his friends began to request their drinks "the Negroni way". A classic was born.

Unlikely as it seems this story is almost certainly true. Count Negroni certainly existed. He led a colourful life, having been a cowboy and a professional gambler in the United States in his youth.

The fame of his invention spread beyond Florence and it became the favourite drink of the Italian Futurists, the avant-garde literary and artistic movement led by Filippo Tommaso Marinetti. Along with many other gin cocktails from the great cocktail age of the 1920s, the Negroni has now become ultra-fashionable again. Partly that is to do with its authenticity, partly too because, like the Martini, it's a drinker's drink. As Kingsley Amis, one of alcohol's great heroes, said: "This is a really fine invention. It has the power, rare with drinks and indeed with anything else, of cheering you up."

The recipe could not be simpler:

Equal parts of gin, Campari and Italian red vermouth such as Martini Rosso. Combine all the ingredients in a mixing glass filled with ice. Stir gently and pour into an old-fashioned glass. Add a hefty orange slice as a garnish.

Although there is no doubt that cocktails are quintessentially American, there has always been a tradition of making mixed drinks in Britain that goes back to Victorian times. Although of course they weren't called cocktails but rather daisies, flips, fizzes, cobblers, slings, punches and many other terms.

GRAPEFRUIT GIN FIZZ

The Fizz is very much in the Collins family in that it is served in a tall glass and includes a carbonated mixer.

50 ml gin
75 ml ruby grapefruit juice
Splash of club soda
Garnish

Pour gin into a tall glass with large cubes of ice. Add ruby grapefruit juice and top with soda water. Garnish with a wedge of ruby grapefruit.

RIGHT: *A Grapefruit Gin Fizz is a delicious combination of bubbly, tart and sweet.*

THE MONKEY GLAND

The Monkey Gland cocktail was created in the 1920s by the famous Harry MacElhone, owner of Harry's New York Bar in Paris. The drink's name was inspired by the experiments of surgeon Serge Voronoff who had invented a technique of grafting monkey testicle tissue on to the testicles of men to boost virility.

40 ml gin
20 ml orange juice
1 teaspoon grenadine syrup
1 dash absinthe
Orange peel for garnish

Mix all ingredients in a shaker. Garnish with orange peel.

THE SIDECAR

Also known as the Chelsea Sidecar to differentiate it from the original recipe traditionally made with cognac, it is believed to have been invented around the end of World War I, in either London or Paris. The Sidecar was named for the motorcycle passenger seat. It's a kind of daisy cocktail.

50 ml gin
20 ml Triple Sec, such as Cointreau
20 ml lemon juice

Mix all the ingredients together and serve.

ABOVE: *Whether the Monkey Gland experiment worked or not, the cocktail has been popular for almost a century.*

BELOW: *The Basil Smash
is a simple mixture of
lemon, sugar syrup,
basil leaves and gin.*

NEW WAVE COCKTAILS

The modern craft cocktail revolution has generated some
splendid new-style cocktails that make the most of fresh fruits,
herbs and even vegetables.

BASIL SMASH

(If you are ever in Hamburg you will
find one of the best bars in the world, Le
Lion, run by Joerg Meyer who invented
this delicious drink.)

60 ml gin
1 lemon
20 ml sugar syrup
6–8 large basil leaves

Cut a lemon in half and squeeze
the juice into a shaker. Throw in the
squeezed lemon as well. Add basil leaves
and muddle. Fill the shaker with ice
cubes. Shake vigorously. Strain into a
tumbler filled with fresh ice.

THE BRAMBLE

(Invented by Dick Bradsell, a pioneer of the London craft
cocktail movement.)

50 ml gin
25 ml freshly squeezed lemon juice
12.5 ml shot sugar syrup
12.5 ml shot crème de mure

Shake the first three ingredients over ice and strain into an
old-fashioned glass filled with crushed ice. Slowly drizzle the
crème de mure through the crushed ice to create a "marbled"
effect and garnish with blackberries and a lemon slice.

EARL GREY MARTEAINI

(The creation of Audrey Saunders, the first lady of American cocktails.)

45 ml Earl Grey tea-infused gin
25 ml freshly squeezed lemon juice
30 ml simple syrup
1 egg white

Shake ingredients hard for 10 seconds. Strain into a chilled cocktail glass that is half-rimmed with sugar. Garnish with a lemon twist.

For the Earl Grey infusion, measure four tablespoons of loose Earl Grey tea into a litre bottle of gin. Cap and shake, and leave for two hours. Strain through a fine sieve into a bowl. Rinse out bottle to remove loose tea, and pour infusion back into clean bottle.

190 ROYALE

This is a version of the old standard Sloe Royale.

50 ml gin
25 ml sloe gin
Mint leaves
2 wedges lime
Sugar syrup
25 ml fresh lemon juice
Champagne or Prosecco

Take a few mint leaves and the lime wedges, and muddle with a dash of sugar syrup. Add the lemon juice, and top up with crushed ice. Add the gin and sloe gin, then stir. Top with Champagne or Prosecco and serve in a Collins glass.

ABOVE: *Earl Grey tea has the aroma of bergamot, a botanical sometimes used in the distillation of gin.*

PUNCHES AND SHARING DRINKS

Punch, a very Victorian drink immortalized by Charles Dickens, has recently made a comeback, particularly during the winter months when nothing is quite as comforting as a bowl of sweet, fragrant, alcohol-infused cheer. As Dickens writes in *David Copperfield*, even the task of making punch is a pleasure.

"Punch, my dear Copperfield, like time and tide, waits for no man … His recent despondency, not to say despair, was gone in a moment. I never saw a man so thoroughly enjoy himself amid the fragrance of lemon-peel and sugar, the odour of burning spirit, and the steam of boiling water, as Mr Micawber did that afternoon. It was wonderful to see his face shining at us out of a thin cloud of these delicate fumes, as he stirred, and mixed, and tasted, and looked as if he were making, instead of a punch, a fortune for his family down to the latest posterity."

DICKENSIAN PUNCH

BELOW: *A warming winter drink, served in tea-cups, this punch was a favourite of Charles Dickens.*

The word "punch" comes from the Sanskrit for "five" as the drink was originally made with five ingredients: alcohol, sugar, lemon, water, and tea or spices. Punch was introduced to England by sailors and employees of the British East India Company in the early 17th century. It was a popular drink in Victorian times and was by all accounts a drink that the great chronicler of the Victorian age, Charles Dickens, himself took great pleasure in making and serving at home.

150 ml gin
1 litre of good-quality hoppy ale
200 ml cloudy apple juice
5 slices of satsuma
1 cinnamon stick
90g sugar
5g hops
2 cloves
1 dessert spoon honey
2 large splashes of Angostura Bitters
1 whole star anise

Heat ingredients all in a pan. Simmer for 20 minutes then strain the hops out and serve with satsuma slices and a stick of cinnamon to garnish. For six people.

ARIZONA BREEZE

Making cocktails at home for a crowd can be time-consuming but drinks like the gin version of the Sea Breeze can easily be made up in quantities.

65 ml gin
75 ml cranberry juice
50 ml grapefruit juice

These basic proportions can be used to make a jug of ready-to-serve cocktails by multiplying as necessary. Add ice to glasses as you serve.

SUMMER COOLER

Based on jug serving six medium tumblers.

200 ml gin
75 ml of elderflower cordial or liqueur
Club soda or ginger ale
Lemon
Garnish: summer fruits

Pour gin over ice into the pitcher. Add the elderflower cordial or liqueur. Top with club soda or ginger ale and garnish with a squeeze of lemon and summer fruits.

GIN PLACES

Until recently, if you wanted to see gin being made and explore its fascinating history in detail, the options were limited. Now, however, no matter where you are, you won't be far from a distillery visitor centre where you can enjoy tours and tastings and, in some cases, even make your own gin. In some places you'll probably be able to see whisky being made too.

Here are just a few of the best gin places. It is by no means a comprehensive list and many of the smaller gin producers actively welcome visitors. Check locally for details.

- BEEFEATER DISTILLERY AND VISITOR CENTRE:
  20 Montford Place, London SE11 5DE
  Book at www.beefeatervisitorcentre.co.uk
- THE BOMBAY SAPPHIRE DISTILLERY:
  Laverstoke Mill, Laverstoke, Whitchurch,
  Hampshire RG28 7NR
  Book at www.bombaysapphire.com
- BRAMLEY & GAGE:
  C6, Ashville Park, Short Way, Thornbury,
  Bristol, South Gloucestershire BS35 3UU
  Book at www.bramleyandgage.co.uk
- BURLEIGH'S GIN:
  The Collection Yard, Bawdon Lodge Farm,
  Charley Road, Leicestershire LE12 9YE
  Book at www.burleighsgin.com
- CITY OF LONDON DISTILLERY:
  22–24 Bride Lane, London EC4Y 8DT
  Book at bookings@cityoflondondistillery.com
- THE COTSWOLDS DISTILLERY:
  Phillip's Field, Whichford Road, Stourton,
  Shipston-on-Stour, Warwickshire CV36 5HG
  Book at www.cotswoldsdistillery.com

- EAST LONDON DISTILLERY:
  221 Grove Road, Bow Wharf, London
  E3 5SN
  Book at tours@eastlondonliquorcompany.com
- THE GINSTITUTE:
  The Portobello Star, 171 Portobello Road,
  London W11 2DY
  Book at www.theginstitute.com
- HAYMAN'S DISTILLERY:
  70 Eastways Park, Witham, Essex
  CM8 3YE
  Book at www.haymansgin.com
- THE LAKES DISTILLERY:
  Setmurthy, near Bassenthwaite Lake,
  Cumbria CA13 9SJ
  Book at www.lakesdistillery.com
- LANGLEY DISTILLERY:
  Crosswells Road, Oldbury, West Midlands
  B68 8HA
  Tours can be arranged by appointment on
  0121 552 1246

- THE LONDON DISTILLERY COMPANY:
  33 Parkgate Road, London SW11 4NP
  Book at www.londondistillery.com
- THE OXFORD ARTISAN DISTILLERY:
  Old Depot, South Park, Cheney Lane,
  Oxford OX3 7QJ
  Book at www. spiritoftoad.com
- PLYMOUTH GIN DISTILLERY:
  60 Southside Street, The Barbican,
  Plymouth, Devon PL1 2LQ
  Book at www.plymouthgin.com
- SIPSMITH DISTILLERY:
  83 Cranbrook Road, London W4 2LJ
  Book at www.sipsmith.com

SCOTLAND AND IRELAND
- CAORUNN GIN:
  Balmenach Distillery, Balmenach Road,
  Cromdale, Grantown-on-Spey PH26 3PF
  Book at www.caorunngin.com
- COLONSAY GIN:
  Gin Lover's Retreats, Isle of Colonsay PA61 7YR
  Book at www.wildthymespirits.com/gin-lovers-retreat/the-experience
- DAFFY'S GIN:
  Strathmashie Distillery, Strathmashie,
  Newtonmore PH20 1BU
  Book at www.daffysgin.com
- DARNLEY'S GIN:
  Kingsbarns Distillery, Kingsbarns,
  St. Andrews, Fife KY16 8QE
  Book at www.kingsbarnsdistillery.com
- THE ECHLINVILLE DISTILLERY:
  62 Gransha Road, Kirkubbin, near Belfast,
  BT22 1AJ
  Book at www.echlinville.com
- EDEN MILL DISTILLERY & BREWERY:
  Main Street, Guardbridge, St. Andrews, Fife
  KY16 0UU
  Book at www.edenmill.com

- ISLE OF HARRIS DISTILLERY:
  Tarbert, Isle of Harris, HS3 3DJ
  Book at www.harrisdistillery.com
- THE LISTOKE DISTILLERY:
  Drogheda, Ireland
  Book at listokedistillery.ie/gin-school
- ORO GIN:
  The Dalton Distillery, Meikle Dyke,
  Dalton. Nr Lockerbie, Dumfries and
  Galloway DG11 1DU
  Book at www.orogin.co.uk
- PICKERING'S GIN:
  Summerhall Distillery, Summerhall Place,
  Edinburgh EH9 1QH
  Book at www.pickeringsgin.com/
- SHETLAND DISTILLERY COMPANY:
  Saxa Vord Distillery, Unst, Haroldswick,
  Shetland Islands ZE2 9EF
  Book at www.shetlandreelgin.com
- VERDANT SPIRIT CO:
  Edward Street Mill, Forest Park Place,
  Dundee DD1 5NT
  Book at www.verdantspirits.co.uk

And if you ever find yourself in the Low
Countries, the birthplace of genever, gin's
ancestor, these two places are must visits:
- JENEVER MUSEUM:
  Witte Nonnenstraat 19, 3500 Hasselt,
  Belgium.
  According to history, the town that invented
  genever so lots of wonderful historical stuff.
  Book at www.jenevermuseum.be/nl
- MUSEUM OF JENEVER:
  Lange Haven 74-76, 3111 CH Schiedam,
  Netherlands.
  Situated in the docks area of the Netherlands'
  genever town, it's crammed with interesting
  information and has a working distillery.
  Book at www.jenevermuseum.nl

GERALDINE COATES, aka Madame Gin, has been writing about gin for more than 20 years and has herself played a significant role in the great gin revival. She has worked closely with a number of major gin brands as a consultant and on training programmes, and now teaches the world's first accredited Gin Diploma. She is also the editor of the world's first website devoted to gin, www.gintime.com.

PICTURE CREDITS